I Was My Mother's Bridesmaid

Advance Praise for
I Was My Mother's Bridesmaid

"The Carlisle sisters and their peers will make you cry, they will make you laugh, and they will make you think—this book is invaluable for both young people and adults."

CLAUDIA BLACK, M.S.W., PH.D, author of *It Will Never Happen To Me*

"This book is a wise breath of much needed air! It takes any shame out of growing up in a blended family and is direct from the hearts of two remarkable young women."

SARK, artist and author of *Succulent Wild Woman*

"A delightfully heart touching and consciousness raising book. Cheers to Erica and Vanessa!"

DAPHNE ROSE KINGMA, author of *The Future of Love*

"With wisdom born of experience Erica and Vanessa give us a kids-eye view of blended family life. Each member of a stepfamily can gain insight and help from their fresh perspective."

SUE PATTON THOELE, author of the *The Courage to Be a Stepmom*

"Erica and Vanessa have written a book that is not only easily readable and universally applicable for parents and young people, it is profound, insightful and thorough."

JORDAN PAUL, PH.D., co-author of *When I Say No I Feel Guilty*

"This book helps divorcing parents put self-defeating guilt aside and focus on the essentials that will truly help their children survive and thrive through the transitions of divorce and remarriage. There is hope; Erica and Vanessa show us exactly where to find it."

CARMEN RENEE BERRY, co-author of *girlfriends: Invisible Bonds, Enduring Ties*

I Was My Mother's Bridesmaid

Young Adults Talk About Thriving in a Blended Family

Erica Celeste Carlisle
and
Vanessa Dawn Carlisle

WILDCAT CANYON PRESS
A Division of Circulus Publishing Group, Inc.
Berkeley, California

I Was My Mother's Bridesmaid: Young Adults Talk About Thriving in a Blended Family

Editorial Director: Roy M. Carlisle
Copyeditor: Priscilla Stuckey
Cover Design: Eleanor Reagh
Interior Design: Terragraphics
Interior Illustrations: Vanessa Carlisle
Typesetting: Terragraphics
Typographic Specifications: Body text set in Goudy 11/14. Headers are TriplexBold.

Printed in the United States of America

Library of Congress Cataloging-in-Publication Data
Carlisle, Erica Celeste, 1976-
    I was my mother's bridesmaid : young adults from blended families tell it like it is / by Erica Celeste Carlisle and Vanessa Dawn Carlisle.
        p.   cm.
    ISBN 1885171-34-X (alk. paper)
    1. Stepfamilies—United States.   I. Carlisle, Vanessa Dawn, 1979-.
    II. Title.
HQ759.92.C36   1999
306.874—dc21   99-31412
                                                                    CIP

Distributed to the trade by Publishers Group West
10 9 8 7 6 5 4 3 2 1

Contents

To our whole blended family,
thank you for giving us the stories we have to tell.
And especially to Mom and Dad,
because you listened to us from the beginning.

Author's Note: We have changed names and
circumstances in order to protect the privacy of our
contributors and their blended families.

A Word from a Parent

In sociological terms blended families are the new lifestyle on the block. We know about large families, small families, extended families, even fatherless families, but until recent history, family trees that looked like several trees superimposed on one another were relatively unheard of. My own parents divorced in the 1950s. I was one of the only kids in my class from a divorced home. Statistics tell us that in the 1990s, four short decades later, many of the kids in my children's classes will come from divorce and most of those will go on to become part of a blended family. When families separate and come together again in totally new configurations, roles that were once a given are forever changed. For the children and their parents "the earth moves under their feet."

As a psychologist working with divorce and as a child of divorce myself, I have struggled with all of the issues that accompany both breaking a family apart and reassembling a new one. There is only one conclusion I can come to that seems to fit this day and age when divorce and remarriage seem here to stay. That is: If we do not give our children a good family—we owe them a good divorce. If, as a society, we now accept and tolerate divorce as mainstream and support people who are not happy together in breaking up the children's home and starting over again, there is one thing that we cannot tolerate or support.

That is a rancorous, antagonistic divorce in which children are literally guaranteed to suffer deeply.

That is where this book comes in. In a gentle, insightful, witty, and brilliant manner, Erica and Vanessa tell their stories and the stories of countless others. In my opinion, this is a "how to" book on divorce and remarriage, a manual on how to create a blended family that works. With a delicate hand, they touch on all of the issues from "what happened to my bedroom" to "who am I in this new world." They take the reader by the hand through the complicated corridors of rebuilding a life, telling us, by example, what works and what doesn't. This is sensitivity training for parents in understanding the experience of the child and will make every child of a blended family feel that someone out there understands— they are not crazy after all. In Seth's story, he talks about the fishing rod his dad gave him at the end of their visit as his "insurance policy that I'd come up to see him again." Rebecca talks about how "we had to get to know each other again every summer because I was changing a lot." "We need our families to try to understand, not pretend the other household doesn't exist," say Erica and Vanessa. When parents deny the other household due to their own unresolved pain, they deny their children half of their heart.

On the lighter side, blended families can still have happy endings. Learning that life can fall apart and be put back together again can reassure us that life has the power to restore and rebuild itself both in its simplest and most complex ways. Serena remembers that "my mom always had this old, decrepit answering machine that only sometimes worked. My stepdad is an attorney, and he needs to actually hear his messages. Three days ago I called and they had just gotten voicemail hooked up. I left this message for them: 'I am feeling betrayed. I am feeling marginalized. I am feeling unimportant; I said you needed this for eight years and you never listened.' It was really funny; I told her that her outgoing message should say, "Serena was right all along; leave a message after the beep." On a more profound level, Zoe reports that her mother and father both became better parents after they remarried, because they were happier people.

This is an important book. It opens up a subject that needs opening up from the inside out. Best written by "experts" who learned to live well and thrive within the blended family system; this book, at times disarmingly practical and beautifully tuned into a kid's reality, at times moving, at times hysterically funny, shows us how to come out whole and okay at the end of the day. It is the most hopeful and optimistic material I've read in a long time on this very little talked about subject that affects so many. As Erica and Vanessa tell us, what you learn when confronted with these issues is to "love more deliberately." Loving more deliberately is what this book is about.

— *Tian Dayton, Ph.D., TEP*

Preface

Our parents filed for divorce when we were ages four and one. From that point on, we grew up commuting between two homes. When our mom remarried and had another child, we became the quintessential "blended family." Divorce, stepparent, half sibling, two homes, two lives, the works. It wasn't ever easy—we often wished for our own private helicopter—but today we are both hardworking college students who love all our family members. We turned out just fine.

We know that many divorced or remarried parents worry about the effects of uprooting their children. No one wants to be from a "broken home." Of course, it would be ideal if every marriage was a happy one, but many are not. The children from these families are not automatically doomed in life. Parents worry that they have somehow "ruined their children's lives forever." But they haven't. Stepparents new to the family worry that they will be immediately hated because of their step status. They won't. We found in talking to our peers that the most important factor in how people get along is not their degree of genetic relatedness but how they treat each other. So what is the best way to treat new stepchildren? How do children adapt to their new Insta-Families? These are the questions we asked.

Our goal is to help children of blended families use their own experiences to provide guidelines for what makes a complex family work well. Who can tell the story of a family better than the child who was raised in it? Here is a chance for parents to get the inside scoop on how reorganized family structures have affected us, now that we are old enough to articulate how we feel. We asked our interviewees to tell us about their families' strengths and flaws and to tell us what helped them survive the chaos.

The voices in this book did not come from a random survey. We are not describing the norm in American blended families, nor are we claiming that ours is the only story to be told. The stories come from a network of people who, despite many obstacles, thrived in their blended families and came through with flying colors. We chose to interview these people because we wanted to tell a story of hope. Our book is full of hard-earned success stories in order to model what has worked, not to generalize about what usually happens. By making these lives public examples, we hope ultimately to lend a compass to other families navigating their own rocky territory. If anything, we want this book to be a banner that reads, "If we could do it, you can, too!"

Of course, no two families are the same. It is important to keep in mind that this is not exactly a how-to book of stepparenting. After all, we have never been parents, we have only been kids. This book grew out of conversations with a family friend who was about to get married and become a stepmother. She wanted a book with advice from people who had actually been there, recently. On the "Stepparenting" shelf in your local bookstore, you will find a bunch of books on this topic with boring covers written by clinical psychologists. They are experts (have they even been in a stepfamily?). Our book is something else entirely.

What we have to offer are our own memories of how we felt, and how we think we have been affected by the blended families where we grew up. We were interested in what adult children from blended families like us had to say about their experiences, and now we want to share their wisdom. You will not read here about the latest findings in large studies, but you will hear real people talking—people who have been there and who still have a sense of humor.

— *Erica Carlisle & Vanessa Carlisle*
Portland, Oregon

Introduction

I n 1990, about one in five children under eighteen in the United States did not live with both biological parents. Of married-couple family households, 5.3 million contained at least one stepchild under eighteen, up from 3.9 million in 1980.[1] Now, almost ten years later, the numbers are even higher. Census figures are interesting, but they do not capture the full complexity of many family systems. There is no column for "Children who live with a single father in one house and a mother and stepfather in a second house" or "Children who live with a redivorced single mother and an older half brother who is like a father." The sheer number of unique, complicated family setups is mind-boggling, but they do have one thing in common. They all require forging new family bonds with outsiders.

Blended families live in every imaginable configuration: with parents, stepparents, siblings, half siblings, stepsiblings, and sometimes all of the above. But additional family members are only the first part of what makes living in a blended family so complicated. Divorce means that many children split their time between more than one household, which requires planning, communication, and compromising by everyone involved. We build family

---

[1] U.S. Bureau of the Census, Current Population Reports, P23-180, *Marriage, Divorce, and Remarriage in the 1990s* (Washington, DC: U. S. Government Printing Office, 1992), 9–13.

relationships through day-to-day contact and interactions, so it is hard to deal with part-time family members, whether or not you are the one doing the traveling. Furthermore, different households have different rules and expectations, which often requires drastic readjustment for the kids who live in them. In the words of one interviewee, seventy miles can seem like the difference between the East Coast and the West Coast.

For some people, describing a complex family system to friends, school administrators, and sometimes other distant family members can be a chore. When people ask us, Vanessa and Erica, where we're from, we still tend to simplify the answer to just "California," to avoid spending ten minutes explaining how we both grew up in Berkeley, then commuted from Los Gatos to Berkeley, and then spent high school in separate houses when Vanessa moved to southern California with our mom and Erica stayed in northern California with our dad. See, it's messy, and people want simple, clean answers. Blended families are anything but simple.

Our numbers are growing, and yet, despite the commonality of such family forms today, there is still a prevailing intuition that children raised in "broken homes" will not "turn out as well," namely, that we are more likely to drop out or do poorly in school, to have behavior or social problems, to become delinquents, and to eventually become divorce statistics ourselves. People associate divorced, single, and remarried parents with lower incomes, instability, and domestic tension. These views developed when divorce and remarriage occurred only under the most desperate circumstances; the question is whether they hold any water today. Are step-families really more prone to develop problems?

Unfortunately, many researchers have shown that there is an empirical difference between original, two-biological parent families and stepfamilies.[2] The differences are small but reliable: children raised in step-families have lower scores on measures of academic achievement, conduct/behavior, psychological adjustment, self-esteem, and social relations.[3] Of course, this difference is between two averages. Many individual children from blended families score better than the average two-parent child, and plenty of two-parent children score below the average for blended family children. But that is little consolation to parents and stepparents.

There is much speculation, theorizing, and research on the reasons for this difference. Clearly, much more work will have to be done before we begin to understand which factors are involved, although with such a complex social phenomenon, we will never know everything. It is impossible to get a prescription for a happy family by walking into a family counselor's office and asking, "What should I do?" because knowing what happens with large averages is only marginally helpful when dealing with

---

[2] Alan Booth and Judy Dunn, eds., *Stepfamilies: Who Benefits? Who Does Not?* (Hillsdale, NJ: Lawrence Erlbaum Associates, 1994), 233.

[3] Paul R. Amato, "The Implications of Research Findings on Children in Stepfamilies" in *Stepfamilies,* 81–87.

special individual cases. However, we cannot neglect the millions of people now living in blended families just because we have no easy answers for them.

No one is taught how to be a good stepparent; no one makes it her life goal to have stepchildren; no one knows what role a third parent has in a child's life. Millions of people face these dilemmas without guidance or the benefit of shared wisdom and experience. We may not be all-knowing experts with the recipe for domestic perfection in hand, but there is something we can do. We can talk about and share our experiences. Parents must understand that they are not alone, that they are perfectly capable of raising their children under complex circumstances, and that their divorce and remarriage can be of great benefit to their children. There does not have to be a gap between children of blended families and other children.

In this book we open that dialogue by sharing the experiences of some young adults, mostly aged eighteen to twenty-five, who grew up in blended families. The stories are diverse in many details, and yet there are common threads as well. Some people met their stepparents as infants and view them as full-fledged parents, some met them as teenagers or adults and view them as a special adult friend. There are sad stories, too, and confessions about more than one heated argument that could be attributed to adolescent crankiness rather than dislike for another person. The children in this book have grown up and left home, which gives us a more objective perspective. Everyday irritations such as a locked bath-room door or a mess left in the kitchen no longer prevent us from seeing how precious our families are.

We start with memories of the new beginnings: recol-lections of our parents' boyfriends and girlfriends, wedding stories, meeting new brothers and sisters, and moving into new homes. These memories of sometimes awkward moments are important because they bring up the issue of a family's history together. Marriage is sup-posed to be a bond that doesn't break, so it can be a trying situation when the children in a family have been around longer than a spouse! For this reason, the bulk of the book is centered around "life after the second wedding," when the changes inside and outside really surface. New names and new houses are one thing, but new people mean not only creating new relationships, but also changing exist-ing ones. Above all, we found that amid the changing relationships and power struggles, people who treat one another respectfully can get along productively.

That finding should reassure us, but a rocky road still stretches ahead. The problems associated with living in a blended family will not diminish that easily. We still have to travel constantly, split up holidays, and sort out confus-ing financial and legal issues, to mention a few. All the stories in this book have a basically similar ending though. We survived. Whether our families supported us, or we found a way on our own, we have thrived. Our sto-ries are characterized by resilience, by flexibility, and by strength. They are your stories, too.

Part One

The Strangers Enter

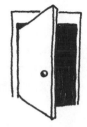

Christmas vacation, 1986. Erica was ten years old and Vanessa was seven. We received a phone call at our dad's apartment from our mother who was on a trip with Jim, whom she had been dating for six years. It went something like this: "Hi girls, we have some news to tell you! We're getting married in a couple of hours!" We were shocked. Sure, they had been engaged twice before, and Jim was one of our best buddies, but they were eloping! *We would not get to be flower girls!*

Of course, as we got older, we had many more reactions to the changes that marriage brought to our lives. But a blended family has to start somewhere. Parents wonder how bringing new people into their lives will affect their children. It is important to understand children's reactions to such new beginnings. As children who have been there, we have a lot of stories to tell.

We begin with the dating scene, with the single parents' romantic trials and errors, and the way those temporary connections affect us as younger children. Girlfriends and boyfriends are connected to our parents by choice and to us by circumstance. They help us develop a certain savvy about what we think our parents need, and in so doing they help us get to know our parents better. Our impressions of their partnerships help shape how we conduct ourselves in our own relationships. When a parent decides to remarry, his or her old boyfriends or girlfriends are a memory archive of traits, habits, and idiosyncrasies that we use to size up the new person.

A wedding always symbolizes a new family alliance. Remarriage means that the new spouses now have an official title that connects them to us: stepparents. What does that new title really signify? There are no easy answers. It can threaten our top-priority position in the family. It can mean we'll finally have a father figure, a mother, two parents. It can mean we now have three or four. Whether the act of remarriage excites us, annoys us, alienates us, or is just plain inconsequential, what matters is how much we are included, how much we want to be involved, and what the new marriage will mean for us individually.

Often remarriage means moving to a new home, sometimes with other children with whom we are supposed to have an instant sibling relationship. Both moving and getting to know new siblings take adjustment. Remarriage can also lead to forging a new routine in an old house, where we have to change our traditions and habits to compromise with someone we haven't lived with before. Learning to live in the same home with a new adult and interacting with stepsiblings helps us redefine who is in "my family." This process takes effort, flexibility, and time. Dating, marrying, moving. It is not always that simple, which is why we delve into all of these new beginnings, discover how they affect us, show the range of our different experiences, and pay tribute to the energy it takes to survive the changes gracefully.

Breakfast with the Boyfriend/ Curlers in the Bathroom

Quiz Question

You are a parent, and your ten-year-old son hates your new girlfriend. You should:

a. Send your child to boarding school
b. Ignore the problem and everything will be fine
c. Talk to your kid, find out why he is upset, make sure he knows he's not being replaced
d. Tell your girlfriend that your son has a rare social disorder and bribe the kid into silence with a new puppy

▼ ▼ ▼ ▼ ▼ ▼ ▼ ▼ ▼ ▼ ▼ ▼ ▼ ▼ ▼ ▼ ▼ ▼

(Answer to quiz at end of section)

There is no etched-in-stone set of rules that say how parents' boyfriends and girlfriends ought to relate to the children. They may become mentors, special older friends, or terrible thorns in our sides, or they may remain phantoms in the background of our parents' lives as mysterious people we never see. Some of them are temporary, some are possible permanent additions, and some take one look at the kids in the house and run out the door screaming in fear. (Often, they are easily intimidated by children.) Each relationship is different because each child is different. When parents' partners are genuine and candid, and make an effort to get to know us individually, the relationship can be mutually rewarding. They give us the opportunity to learn lessons that we can't learn from our parents alone because they bring with them new histories, new experiences, and new expertise. We, in turn, give them permission to be part of the family.

Aside from what we learn from the girlfriends and boyfriends directly, during the dating process we are constantly gaining new information about our parents. Parents have to juggle both the responsibilities of having children and the new freedom of being a "swinging single." We watch them maneuver through the dating world, compromise with their partners, and grieve losing love— all while raising a child. Through our observations, we both develop a model of how to deal with similar situations ourselves and recognize our parents as real people who can make mistakes. So what exactly do we observe? We remember the blunders, the juggling acts, the good times, and the friends.

Jordan is a twenty-two-year-old college student who escapes town to go camping whenever he can. For him, the men his mother dated were his ticket into the world of outdoor sports. He describes the boyfriend that he enjoyed the most: "He was an educated man, but he wasn't stuffy. He liked the outdoors. He was blown away by how much energy kids have. Since being with children was foreign to him, he didn't know any of those stupid adult tricks or phony ways of being nice to kids; he was just himself. We'd play catch with him. He enjoyed playing catch, and it wasn't because he was doing his duty, playing catch with a kid. He just liked that activity; we both liked it, and we got along. Plus, he had an awesome dog."

Meredith, a vivacious nineteen-year-old (who still has a messy room), echoed the appeal of a memorable dog: "When my sister and I were little, my mom lived with a man who didn't like us running in the house, yelling, making big messes and cutting things, which was about all we were into at the time. He had a dog, Shasta, that we loved to wrestle with in the house, but we were never allowed to. I remember a constant battle over whether or not we should be knocking into the table legs and fighting with the dog on the floor. But Shasta liked it, too, so I blame her personally; she was older than us, so she should have been the responsible one! Even though as kids we were a little too rowdy for that boyfriend, now I adore him. He is a funny, smart, cultured, and interesting man."

Children can instantly detect someone who feels comfortable around them and knows how to play. That was especially important for Ben, a nineteen-year-old college student, who told us about the girlfriend he liked the most: "She was the first one who tried to connect with us, or at least the first one who actually succeeded. She was really fun, and we always had a good time. I remember her doing yoga and hanging upside down. I always thought that was really funny. She didn't try to be a mother— some other girlfriends thought that was what they were supposed to do. She didn't try to stay in any adult role, she just joked around and played. I was in sixth grade, so that was important!"

Relationships are built on common ground. The girl-friends and boyfriends who connected with us as little children did so because they had the right level of energy—high. Nora, a sophisticated twenty-two-year-old, still gushes about her favorite of her dad's girlfriends: "She was great. She had more energy than anyone I have ever met. It was like she was on methamphetamines all the time, but she wasn't. She was big on gardening and liked going to the track. Normally, she would be running around, dancing, talking to people, throwing things around, and just being a fireball. She was like a big sister. When they broke up, my dad called me—I was twelve years old at the time—and he was crying, just bawling. He told me that he had just found a note. It said she was gone. All her stuff was gone. I said, 'I'm going to get on a plane. I'm going to come up there.' At first he told me not to, but eventually he said okay. So I had my mom help me buy a ticket, and I got on the plane the same afternoon, and I went up to see my dad and iron his shirts and look after the garden and do a little cooking and try to smooth things over. I told him, 'Listen, Dad, she's just a girl. I liked her, too.'" Parents need to remember that often as we are consoling them after a breakup, we are grieving too, and may need some consoling ourselves.

Breakups can be hard on us, especially if we have become attached to our parent's girlfriend or boyfriend. Often, we are asked to break contact completely with someone we care about deeply. Vanessa remembered that she was very upset after one of our dad's girlfriends left. "I loved her. She was beautiful, fun, and always ready to laugh. She had a vivid imagination and liked creative games. I really looked up to her. She and our father were very serious, and I was very excited about having her in my life. Then one day when Dad came to pick up Erica and me for the weekend, we asked where she was, and he told us that they had broken up and that she wasn't coming back. I was devastated. I cried so much, and I blamed him for taking her away from me." These other adults have the potential to influence us greatly, and sometimes that means we learn about heartbreak along with our parents. If children are truly close with a parent's boyfriend or girlfriend, the parent should remain open to allowing them to see each other after the breakup.

When parents' boyfriends and girlfriends generously involve themselves in our lives, sometimes our relationships with them last longer than the ones they had with our parents. Erica remembered how one of our father's girlfriends made a difference in her life: "When I was in high school, we had a fire at the house we lived in with our mom. A lot of my and Vanessa's things were ruined.

We had no sheets and no lamps. Many of our clothes and toys were water-damaged, as were the posters on the walls and books on our shelves. Everything smelled like wet ashes. Tamara, our dad's girlfriend at the time, took us both on an elaborate shopping spree to replace what we had lost and to pamper us a bit after such a hard time. She came over to the house, our mother's house, and helped us clean up what we could. Her support and sense of humor helped us through a very difficult experience. Vanessa and I both love and respect her and are close with her years after her relationship with our father ended."

As we get older, the boyfriends and girlfriends we like the most are the ones who make our parents happy. We are able to see that our parents need companionship and love, and so we appreciate the people who can give it to them, regardless of whether they become close friends of ours. Rosa, nineteen, was in high school when her parents divorced, and she thinks their new relationships are more satisfying for them. "My mom has been seeing a man that she met through a personal ad. He takes her out to see a lot of plays. When my mom and dad were married, my dad was a workaholic, so he was very tired when he got home, and they didn't talk much. She needed someone to hang out with her, and her new boyfriend does that." Rosa also told us why she approves of her father's new girlfriend. "My dad is your typical absentminded professor. We talk about him from a foot away and he does not notice. She made an attempt to get to know me without forcing things. She's funny; she chats. She's interested in my life. And they are certainly happy. I've never seen him happier."

As older kids, we notice whether or not the relationships improve our parents' lives, because that is more important than how they will affect us directly. Ben jokingly explained why his dad is happy with his current girlfriend: "They both are similarly twisted and sick! They have a great time being deranged together; they love it. They're both comedians. I think they're very well suited." When we are older, and especially after we have moved away from home, we are glad when our parents find companions they enjoy, even if their lifestyles surprise us. Jay, an easygoing nineteen-year-old, agrees. He described his mother's current boyfriend, who also happens to be his favorite: "He is almost twenty years younger than my mom, but it's okay with me because he seems great and it makes her happy. I think age is irrelevant. He doesn't separate us as Adult and Child. He doesn't censor what he talks to me about. He's a person, and we talk." Rosa, Ben, and Jay clearly point out two fundamentals for boyfriends and girlfriends to remember: make our parents happy and talk to us with respect. If either of these requirements are missing, we will notice, and disapprove.

We do not want our parents to be alone, but it hurts if their partnerships develop at our expense. We can feel displaced or ignored if a parent sacrifices crucial time with us for their romance. Serena is a recent college graduate, who is part of a tightly knit family. She told us about her mother's absence during her high school prom: "Her boyfriend felt uncomfortable being around our house, so my mom would leave and fly out to where he lived. Before the prom my junior year I said, 'Mom, the prom's in only a couple weeks, and I'm so excited!' She told me she already had plans to go visit him, and I was very disappointed because I wanted her to be there. She thought we could take our own pictures." Eventually, Serena's mother ended the relationship, and her boyfriend no longer separated her from her children. Single parents have the unique responsibility of weighing the costs and benefits of a new relationship not only for themselves, but also for their children. If they forget to include us, we feel ignored, a boring second best to a new romance.

Similar experiences have led many single parents to realize that their children are part of deciding who goes and who stays. Some even work out an approval system because they discover that their kids are good character judges. Lydia, nineteen, is working to put herself through college. She and her mother established such a system after one very questionable boyfriend. "I could not stand him the first time I met him. I kept telling her that he wasn't good enough for her, but she wouldn't listen. It turned out that he had a police record a mile long, and all I could say was 'I told you so.' From then on she did not dismiss what I said, because I tended to be right. She would introduce me to somebody, and if I didn't like him, she wouldn't date him."

The approval system requires a great deal of communication between parent and child, which will have the positive result of bringing them closer together. Of course, sharing the details of their private lives can backfire on parents, because children aren't always good at keeping secrets. Rebecca, twenty-eight, now has an infant daughter of her own. She told us that as a little girl she once blew her mother's cover. "My grandmother came over for dinner. I was five or six years old, and I said, 'Gosh, it's so great, we got to have Daniel over for breakfast and you over for dinner!' My grandmother said, 'Really? Breakfast. Mmmmmm.' He had spent the night, but I didn't know that. My grandmother inferred it, and my mom was very embarrassed." Nora also remembers inadvertently creating a sticky situation for her father: "When I was about thirteen, my father and I met Christine while we were in the city together. She really liked me. She gave me a scarf at the end of the evening, a scarf I still have. The awful part is that my father's girlfriend at the time, Susan, was away on a trip. Christine came home with us and spent the night. It didn't occur to me that it would upset Susan. When Susan got back, it was the scarf that gave it away, so I felt like the fight was my fault. I got my father in trouble, and I made Susan really unhappy. We went out to dinner, and I tried to smooth things over." Children are not renown for their tact, usually because they don't realize there are any beans to spill! There is probably not much that can be done to prevent such mishaps; they just come with the territory of being a parent.

For our part, our favorite thing about interfering in our parents' private lives is that we get to joke about them. Nina gave us a historical account of her mother's dating life: "She went through phases. There was the pretty boy phase. Then there was a phase where she dated tow truck drivers and Hell's Angels. She still does that every once in a while. She's friends with a lot of Hell's Angels now. Then she went through this 'furry' stage. That's what I call it, because all the guys she dated seemed really furry to me. They had long hair. They had beards. They had sideburns. I could never tell any of them apart." The boyfriends and girlfriends who don't stick around very long usually become a blur to us, getting lumped into various categories in our memories. Meredith poked fun at her father: "He had a lot of blonds, as I recall, one of whom had a small poodle that I was scared of. However, she also had a wading pool, so she was all right." Meredith likes to describe old boyfriends and girlfriends in caricature. "Mom had a boyfriend that we lived with for a while who made us walk on tip-toes. I've met his son, and he can't put his heels on the ground. But," she quipped, "he is a great soccer player."

Having a parent's girlfriend or boyfriend come through our lives, even if it is only for a short while, gives us an opportunity to look at our parents up close and to learn about relationships in a way that is unique from children with married parents. The boyfriends and girlfriends we liked had a few common characteristics: they made our parents happier, and they made a genuine effort to get to know us individually. We are highly observant judges of character, and feel as though we can spot a bad apple from a mile away. When our parents respect our feelings about their romantic relationships, we are much more likely to enjoy their boyfriend or girlfriend instead of compete with them.

Parents who are new on the dating scene worry that we will grow up afraid to love because we witness their breakups. It doesn't have to be that way. Although we do get hurt, our grief over the loss of a boyfriend or girlfriend does not teach us not to love. In fact, the people our parents date help us learn to love more deliberately, because we see that there is more than one way to show it. And knowing that is the basic glue that holds any blended family together.

The answer to the quiz question is C. By far the best way to deal with a problem is to confront it. Ignoring it will not make it go away (neither will lying about it). Communicating in a sincere, caring way will help get to the bottom of the problem and will also help children feel important and valued.

I Was My Mother's Bridesmaid

▼ ▼ ▼ ▼ ▼ ▼ ▼ ▼ ▼ ▼ ▼ ▼ ▼ ▼ ▼ ▼ ▼

Quiz Question

The man you are about to marry has two loud, opinionated children. You should:

   a. Get married on the sly and not tell them for six months

   b. Get to know them and involve them in the ceremony

c. Pretend they don't exist
d. Smile, grit your teeth, and thank god they won't be coming on the honeymoon

▼ ▼ ▼ ▼ ▼ ▼ ▼ ▼ ▼ ▼ ▼ ▼ ▼ ▼ ▼ ▼ ▼ ▼ ▼

(Answer to quiz at end of section)

When our parents date we get a taste of what it is like to incorporate new people into our lives, but it is when our parents remarry that the blended family really begins. Some children don't realize exactly how much the wedding will continue to affect them after the guests have gone home and the stepparent stays. They are caught up in the details of the moment and do not usually start worrying about how their family will be different until the ceremony is all over. Other children may react more strongly to a marriage announcement because they can grasp the magnitude of the change, and they have a more extensive past to cling to. For those of us who are already grown up when a parent remarries, it is an event that we enjoy for our parent's sake, not for our own. A wedding is a transition to a blended family, whether or not we have left either of our nests.

A wedding is often an event worth remembering, especially when we get to be in our parents' ceremonies! Nora, who took on big responsibilities at a young age, told us about her mother and stepfather's wedding: "They got married when I was about seven. I was the flower girl, and I remember I was so nervous that I forgot to scatter the flower petals. I got up to the preacher and was standing behind my mother when I realized that I still had all the little yellow rose petals. I was so stressed out from that moment on." Weddings themselves take a great deal of time and attention, and we can feel lost in the shuffle. Moms and dads tying the knot: Your children will be more at ease if you reassure them that what is important is that they are there to celebrate with you.

Abigail, a college student and artist, was young when each of her parents remarried. Even though she was the same age at both, she remembers feeling very different at each of her parents' ceremonies. She said of her father's wedding, "I was very crabby the entire time. All the pictures of me show me being really grumpy. I think I felt neglected because I wasn't the center of attention. I didn't really see the point in having a big wedding. We had to camp, and I didn't like camping at the time. I didn't know anyone, and there weren't very many kids my age. Everybody sat in a big circle, they exchanged vows, and we sang some songs. We ate for a while, and that was it." Her memories of her mother's wedding are considerably more agreeable. "There were a lot more kids and fun on my mom's side. It was not a camping trip; it was a party. When I was that age, I liked parties a lot. It was a very simple wedding, but afterward there was a band, lots of fancy food, and dresses. My uncle taught me how to waltz, and we got to stay up late, so I liked that wedding much better." For young children, the wedding ceremony is more about immediate details like cake, a party, and fancy clothes than a symbol of the change from a single-parent household to a blended family.

Denise was older when her mother remarried, and she experienced both the chaos of a wedding and the emotional impact of her family changing. She is twenty-three, works in marketing, and told us that she played the title role in our book. "I was my mom's bridesmaid. They got married in our living room; there was only family there. I wore black! I cried the whole time but I was crying out of total relief. My mom had somebody else! I had felt very responsible for my mom for my whole childhood, so I would be concerned when she was alone. I remember saying when I was ten years old, 'I'm not going to college unless you are married.' I wanted her to be taken care of. When she did get married, I thought my life had turned over 150 percent. Plus, from the outside perspective, my family seemed more normal. She had settled down and found someone to marry her. I was relieved."

As children, we equate a marriage announcement with a ceremony, but as adolescents, teenagers, and twenty-somethings, we know that it means much more than that. We know that real changes will come, and we can imagine how different our lives will be after the vows are exchanged. We don't have to be part of the wedding to be aware of the family's transformation. For Zoe, a lively college student and sculptor, the news that her father was going to remarry meant that her life was going to take a big new turn. She told us that she was entering high school when she met her stepmother and stepsister. "My dad married a woman whom he had known for three weeks before they were engaged. He came to pick me up and told me I was going to meet his future wife today. He gave me a superficial profile of her, and we drove forty-five minutes away to meet this woman and her daughter. They had already worked out the logistics and agreed that she and her daughter, who was also going to be a freshman in high school, would move in with us. We had lunch with them at their house. We sat and talked. It was bizarre." The transition might have been smoother for Zoe if she had been asked how she felt about the changes, instead of being thrown into a situation over which she had no control. Even when parents have made their final decision about marriage, children need to feel that their opinions are being honored.

Derek, nineteen, had a similarly abrupt life change. He explained how his mother's remarriage came as a surprise: "She had gone to work as a paralegal, and she met a lawyer. She came over to my grandmother's house one day, when I had just gotten home from school. The news went basically like this: We're getting married and we're moving to north Florida, so let's go out to dinner and you can meet your new father. I wasn't very happy about it. We went out to dinner. When you're seven years old, you don't usually notice awkwardness in social situations. But I remember that dinner, and I remember feeling very awkward. It made a big impact on me."

When the marriage comes as a complete surprise, it is often more difficult for us to adjust to. Martin, a nineteen-year-old biochemistry major, remembers finding out that his father was leaving his mother to marry someone else: "My father met my stepmother in Russia on a sabbatical. I remember him coming home one day and telling us all that he had met this woman, that he fell in love over in Russia, and that he was leaving. I was confused and didn't understand what was going on. I had no indication that any of that was ever going to happen, because my parents never fought at all. My dad managed to bring my stepmother into the country as a guest, and she obtained her green card by marrying my father." He describes their first meeting: "I remember her being a lot more nervous than I was. She seemed very uneasy being near me. I'm not sure really why; I was just a little eight-year-old boy. I didn't know how intimidating I could be to her." Children who will be living with their stepparent-to-be deserve time to establish a trusting relationship with him or her, so that they do not feel as if their old family arrangement is being taken from them. The transition from girlfriend to fiancée is easier for everyone than the shock of stranger to stepmom.

Sarah, twenty-one, a social activist, was shocked by her mother's marriage announcement. However, her mother made an effort to involve her in the process. When her mother decided to remarry, Sarah was resistant to the idea at first because she didn't know the new man. So her mother arranged for them to meet. "It really surprised me when she called me one day and told me that she was going to get married. I'd heard about the guy she'd been dating, but she had only known him for a couple of months. I said, 'What are you doing? You don't know who this guy is!' I was asking her all kinds of questions, interrogating her. She was already telling me the date for the marriage. She finally decided that she wanted to fly me up there to meet him and let me measure out the situation. She made it seem like I would have some say in it, but it was nearly final. I went up for a weekend in October, and the wedding was already set for November 9. I spent the weekend with him, and I'm sure he was nervous, but it was a good time. I liked him a lot. I could tell that he was really in love with my mom and that he was willing to do anything for her." Even though Sarah knew that the wedding date was set, it is clear that her mother's concern about her opinion helped her to feel more at ease about the marriage. Sarah's mother made a wise choice when she invited her daughter to form her own opinion. Parents must find the balance between doing what they feel is right for their own lives and regarding their children's feelings about their actions. Nowhere is this more important than in picking a spouse.

Kara, who holds a degree in psychology, was asked directly for approval on her mother's plans to marry. She told us, "I was consulted about the marriage. I remember very distinctly being five years old and in the bathtub. My mom came in and said, 'Is it okay if we marry John?' I told her I thought it would be all right. Then it was set. I was very involved in that decision." She was also very excited and accepted her stepfather into her life instantly. "It was 'Daddy-John' in the beginning before they were married, and then when they married—actually at the wedding—I ran up to him, through the aisle, probably disturbed the whole thing, climbed up his front, hugged him, and said, 'I love you, Daddy.' He said it was one of the best moments of his life."

Even when we are not explicitly asked for approval, we like to know we have not been forgotten when a parent brings in a new family member. Nora's father surprised her with his announcement of marriage, but he still let her know he was thinking about her, albeit in an unconventional way. "My father just called me up one day and told me he was getting married the next day. I remember the first time I saw her, he was making dinner. She really likes eggplant. I hate eggplant. It makes me sick. My father was trying to please both of us, so he made eggplant, but he made all the things that I really like on it. He put tomatoes on it, and some goat cheese, and some other really lovely things. He soaked it in balsamic vinegar. After that my father gave me *Love in the Time of Cholera*, a book where one character says to another 'Yes. I'll marry you, as long as you promise never to make me eat eggplant.' Of course, it should have said, 'I'll *let* you marry *her*,' but I never did have to eat eggplant again!"

Children aren't the only ones who have to adjust, but usually we are the most vocal about it. Some of our parents are reluctant to tell us about their decision to remarry, because they are afraid we will have strong negative reactions to the news. Ben remembers that he found out about his parents' divorce and his mother's new fiancé at about the same time, which, incidentally, was after everyone else in his family. "Everybody knew before I did! Finally, they clued me in to what was going on: Dad's been fooling around, so Mom's leaving and she's found a really great Italian guy who is going to love her forever. They thought that I would get the most worked up about it. Actually, I just stepped out for a while, got over it, and played with my blocks again." Tell us important news as soon as possible. If we are going to be upset, we are going to be upset. Delaying the news will only make it worse. Suzanne, a twenty-year-old fitness trainer, was very angry that she didn't know about her father's wedding. "I was talking to a relative one day, and she said, 'I didn't see you at the wedding.' I said, 'What wedding are you talking about?' She said, 'Your dad got married.' I wasn't invited. I called him, and I basically told him where to stick it. He could have told me. It really hurt me that he didn't." Suzanne wasn't upset that her father got married; she was angry that he didn't tell her about it. By failing to tell our families about important events, we do not prevent their angry responses, we just give them more to be angry about.

While the above goes for most people, there are exceptions. When Meredith's mother got married, Meredith didn't find out about it until six months later, but luckily for her mother, Meredith was unaffected by the news. Meredith was in high school and didn't live with her mother when she got married, and the marriage didn't affect her life directly. "She sat down and mentioned that her one-year anniversary was coming up. I said, 'Pardon?' And she said something to the effect of, 'It was kind of an insurance thing . . . we got married,' and I said, 'Do you have a ring?' She showed me this little ring and I said, 'Well. All right, so what's for dinner?' There was a point in time at which Jeff and I realized that this made him my stepdad. We both found that rather amusing and had a good laugh about it. That was it." Meredith's case is actually quite rare. Her story reminds us of the diversity in our experience, and reiterates the fact that different families deal with these issues in very different ways.

Zoe remembers that her mother's wedding was also very underplayed. "We started going house shopping together when the lease was running out on our apartment. We went house shopping with Sean. Sean, at this point, was still my mom's boyfriend. We found a really beautiful house that went on the market the same day as our old house. They got the house together, and they went to Mexico on vacation. When they came back I asked her if they were getting married. They looked at each other, got a little embarrassed and shy, but said yes. They got married in a thirty-second ceremony at the Justice of the Peace office, and we went for brunch."

Most parents can tell how much information we want from them. Generally, the younger we are, the more important it is to us to feel involved in the marriage, because when we are children we are more directly affected by the stepparent. This is not to say that we lose interest just because we grow older. Our families are still our families, whether we are five or twenty-five, and the ways in which they change are meaningful.

For many of us, our new stepparent is someone we have known for quite some time. However, the marriage can significantly change our relationship with them. Meredith's stepmother had been a part of her life for much longer than the duration of the engagement. In fact, Meredith says that her father and stepmother "grew up together like cousins. Actually, when they started dating, it was really bizarre, and it took everyone a while to get used to. My dad, my sister, and I were living together, and she came over to hang out. The kids went to bed (that's me and my sister), and the two of them stayed up for a long time talking. When she went to leave they kissed, and she says it was the weirdest thing that has ever happened to her. She left and didn't call for a week. The next time they saw each other they both realized that this was it: they were going to get married. When we moved in together a couple of months later, they already knew that this probably should have happened all along. After my mom and dad's divorce, both of them went through a lot of boyfriends and girlfriends, so it was nice to have somebody around that I knew."

Whether we understand it at the time or only after our lives visibly change, a remarriage is the beginning of our new family. New spouses are new stepparents, and when they say, "I do" to our parents, they say the same to us. Where and how they fit into our daily lives is the next discovery we have to make.

The answer to the quiz question is B. You are going to be a part of each other's lives for a very long time. A relationship built on avoidance will never be close, but one built on effort and respect has much better chances.

A New Baby!?!

▼ ▼ ▼ ▼ ▼ ▼ ▼ ▼ ▼ ▼ ▼ ▼ ▼ ▼ ▼ ▼ ▼ ▼

You and your new spouse are expecting a baby. You tell your stepchildren that they will:

   a. Not be allowed to baby-sit
   b. Now have to make their own dinner
   c. Remain just as important to you as before
   d. Have to move into the garage

▼ ▼ ▼ ▼ ▼ ▼ ▼ ▼ ▼ ▼ ▼ ▼ ▼ ▼ ▼ ▼ ▼ ▼

(Answer to quiz at end of section)

Most of us were very small, perhaps just twinkles in our mothers' eyes, when our siblings were born, but that is not usually the case with half siblings. We may be ten or even twenty years old when mom or dad remarries and decides to begin a family with the new partner. Having a few years under our belts makes a difference in how we relate to half siblings. The shock when we first learn of their existence is greater, because after several years of ruling supreme, we are just not expecting it! But then, in our maturity, we are able to quickly adjust to the idea, and most of us learn to enjoy the little ones. Some of us who grew up as only children are pleased to finally have a sibling; most of us find it strange to see our parents fawn over a newborn. We like playing with and helping to care for the baby, especially since we do not have to get up with it in the middle of the night. Although we may need a little time to get used to not being the center of attention for a while, we won't hold it against the little ones. Eventually, they win their way into our hearts, and we do not recognize the "half" in front of their names. They are simply our brothers and sisters.

Laura, twenty-three, grew up an only child. She didn't have the usual nine months to adjust to the news of her new sister, and it wasn't easy for her. "I remember I was thirteen and I was sitting at my desk at my mom's house. I got a phone call from my stepmom who told me that she and my dad had adopted a girl. It had all happened within three days. She told me that I had a sister. I said 'Congratulations. That's wonderful; you will make terrific parents.' I hung up the phone and cried and cried in hysterical fits. My mom and stepdad hugged me; they were great. They took me for ice cream, and I remember I had a pound cake sundae that night. Intellectually I knew it was fine, but my dad was going to call somebody else 'pumpkin'! I thought they wouldn't care when I came home to visit. I wasn't going to get the attention that I was used to. I was saying, 'Am I not good enough? Why did they need to have a baby?' My stepdad and mom just shook their heads and gave me total love. My stepdad said to me, 'Laura, like Big Bird always used to say, love isn't like birdseed; there's enough for everybody.' I hated him at that moment; I was probably flipping him off while he said it to me. I had a friend who was also an only child whose mom was pregnant; she was so mad. We would sit and complain, 'Can you believe they are having another kid?' Being an only child is a big deal. I went to my dad's a month later, and I met my sister. I have been thrilled about her ever since."

Even if we aren't particularly surprised to discover that our parents and stepparents are expecting, the experience can still be difficult. When he was eight years old, Martin had struggled to adjust to his father's remarriage. For him, the news of the baby signified that his blended family was an irrevocable fact. "I went over to my dad's house, and he told me that my stepmother was pregnant. After my parents had gotten divorced, I had the notion that maybe they could get back together after a while, and I held on to that hope for some time. But after my stepmother got pregnant, I let the idea go to the ground immediately, for the last time. I remember when the baby was born. He actually looked a lot like me when I was a baby, which was surprising. He is a very smart kid, and he's very nice. I have no hard feelings against him. We actually get along well."

Babies are hard to resist for long, as both Laura and Martin learned. Like Laura, Mark was an only child until a few years ago. Mark's younger half sister was born when he was already away at college, but they are close nonetheless. "She's smart. Maybe I am just saying that because we have a sibling bond, but we have fun conversations, she listens to my music, and we take walks together. We hang out. We'll watch TV or play games, or I'll build things so she can knock them down. She's only two, but we have a relationship. I think it was pretty good timing because I got to be an only kid while I lived there, and the second I left they had another one, so now I have a half sister who is there when I come to visit. I don't have to deal with her day in and day out; I only see her when she is jazzed to see me. When I come home it's like a party, and I really like that role. As far as I am concerned, she's the best thing I've ever seen."

Mark did not feel as threatened at first as Laura did, probably because it is easier to give up our place in the spotlight voluntarily, as we do when we move away to college, than to have it taken from us. Laura described what it is like for her to visit her dad and stepmom now that her half sister is no longer a baby. "I don't mind that I don't get the attention that I used to, but obviously their lives have totally changed. We don't go out. Having an eight-year-old, you can't have long dinners; you can't go to a late movie. Because they have a small child, I see my parents in a way I am not really used to. Plus, they were younger when I was a child, and now I see them parenting differently. When they had me, they would go over to somebody's house and stay up late, having a good time. Now with my sister, they decide they have to be home by nine; the difference between twenty-five-year-old parents and forty-five-year-old parents is huge." We, Erica and

Vanessa, also notice the differences, but they work in our half sister, Kelsey's, favor! "The rules got much less strict for Kelsey. We never let our mom forget that when we were little we were only allowed to watch one hour of TV and chew one piece of gum a day. Kelsey, of course, gets away with several of each."

The difference between young parents and older ones may not be one of changed principles, but changed energy levels: parenting is exhausting work. Parents who have older children are lucky because we are often eager to help change the baby's diapers, feed her mashed carrots, and give her baths. Allison, twenty, still loves collecting comic books, but her dad and stepmom were very glad to have her help when their second baby came along. She told us why: "Corinne actually screamed for the first year of her life, and anybody who was around her in that time can back me up on this. She was horrible. My sister and I called her the Evil Baby. She had colic and then was teething; there was always some reason why Corinne was shrieking at the top of her lungs. We used to call it Tag Team Parenting, because no one person could stand being in a room with her for more than an hour, so we would have to tag somebody else and say, 'Look, you have to hold her because I am going to go crazy if I stay in this room anymore.' The only way that she would even consider any abatement of the screeching was if you were standing, holding her, and walking around—you couldn't even sit and hold her—and half the time she would scream when you were standing anyway. And then she turned one and she was great. She's always had a fire in her." Allison's dad and stepmom relied on her help, and the involvement helped Allison adjust to having a new baby around.

Being involved in taking care of the baby can help us feel more secure about our place in the family. Erica remembers, "When Kelsey was born, my mom told me that before I could take care of the baby myself, she wanted me to take a baby-sitting course. My best friend and I took the class together. It was a joke, but it did boost my confidence. I was pleased that my mom thought I was trustworthy and responsible enough that she could leave the baby with me. Plus, it meant that I was really Kelsey's big sister, not just my mom's other daughter."

Cooperation is the key to a harmonious household, and a baby demands it. Jordan has always been very involved in his half brother's life. When the baby was born, it was a boon to their whole family. "After Andy was born, for a long time things were peaceful because my step-father, who normally had a very quick temper, was always so sweet and good to him. That made my mom happy, which was really nice. We had fun. Andy was something that we all had in common. He pulled us together."

Babies do seem to have a special ability to bring people together, as Sarah also discovered. She was so upset that her dad married her stepmother that she refused to attend the ceremony. But, she confessed, the births of her half siblings have helped ease the situation. "The thing that ultimately allowed me to feel some level of comfort about their marriage was that they had a baby. At first, the news was another traumatic event; I thought, 'Oh, my God, not only is my father in a relationship, but now they are going to start having kids, another whole family.' But I really like babies, so there was no way that I could ignore them anymore. Throughout the whole thing my step-mother was very nice and always tried to reach out to me, but I was just not willing to accept it. I was slowly getting used to someone else in my life and in my father's life. The children really helped. They bring us together." Surprisingly, Sarah wasn't resistant to new siblings. In fact, they helped facilitate her relationship with her stepmom. But that relationship would never have blossomed if Sarah's stepmom had not made the effort to connect with Sarah.

For some of us, the actual birth is more traumatic than learning of the pregnancy or even living with a newborn. Births are always frantic events, and older children may be herded off quickly, causing them anxiety or feelings of desertion. Abigail was ten when her half brother was born, and luckily she remembers the story with a sense of humor. "My mom's water broke while we were eating dessert, and all of a sudden everybody had to get up and go. I wanted to finish my ice cream! My mom called my dad so my sister and I could go over there while she was at the hospital, but he wasn't home. Then her obstetrician was gone for the weekend, so the hospital had to page the on-call obstetrician. Ironically, that obstetrician was a friend of my dad's, and my dad was at her house playing bridge, which was the reason that my mom couldn't get hold of him. That was funny later but not at the time, because we had to go to someone else's house. My sister and I were taken to our friends' place, but no one was home except their grandmother. She smoked a lot and was kind of grim and mean, and she made us go straight to bed. She probably wasn't really mean, but I thought she was mean. I was miserable and I cried a lot. Once my brother was born and we all got home everything was okay. I have always gotten along with him."

Our little half siblings are generally quite good at winning our affections. For Meredith's half brother, the process took a little time. Meredith is now the little boy's biggest fan, and she told us how it happened. "Miles was born a month early, and I was deeply unimpressed with him. I was ten when he was born. He was hideous; I can't even describe how ugly he was. Apparently the last month of a child's in-uterus period is just spent getting cute, and he missed it. He looked like one of those little dead birds that just fell out of the nest. He had this huge nose, he was all red, and all he did was sleep for probably two months. I thought, 'So this is what we waited eight months for? This is stupid.' We never saw him. Sometimes he would cry a little bit, my stepmom would feed him, and then he was asleep again." But babies don't stay newborns, and Miles was no different. Meredith continued, "I actually know the exact moment when I fell in love with Miles; it took about half an hour. He had a little swing that he sat in while my stepmom cooked. He was old enough that he could hold himself up, and he was just becoming aware of the world. I had long hair at the time, and I was standing there squinting at this little thing, thinking, 'You know, we should have just gotten a cat.' And I sneezed. All of my hair, mounds of it because I really have thick hair, flew in front of my face. I don't do a dainty sneeze. And he laughed. He didn't just giggle, he was guffawing. I looked at him, and I thought, 'Wow, this kid is cool!' So I did it again, and I threw all my hair in front of my face, and he kept laughing. I couldn't believe it. So I called my sister Janet over (she had a ton of hair, too), and we stood there for literally half an hour doing this. We'd do it together, or we'd do it one after another, and he was just dying, he was laughing so hard. I think he got hiccups, and finally we had to stop because his stomach was starting to cramp up. In the space of that half hour I fell in love with Miles, and it was definitely different after that. Since that moment it's never been 'Oh, he's my half brother.' He is mine. He is one hundred percent my brother, and if there was some word that meant 'more than brother,' he'd be that. But I don't know one, so brother is the one I use."

The story of Meredith and Miles doesn't end there. Meredith told us another story, demonstrating that she is much more than a sister to him, too. "Miles lost his first tooth. He brought it home, and he showed it to everybody, and we were all impressed, but my parents never did the tooth fairy routine. I never got money, my sister never got it, and I thought that sucked, so I decided to do it for Miles. They had explained to him that there was no tooth fairy and that no money was going to show up under his pillow. Everyone at school had been telling him about it, so it bugged him that he was out of the loop. I told him he should probably put his tooth under the pillow just in case. He finally did after quite a bit of cajoling. After he had passed out (kids don't sleep; they pass out), I put two quarters under his pillow and took the tooth. When he woke up I was standing there waiting to tell him to check, but he said, 'There is no tooth fairy.' He figured I was just lying to him when I told him he should look under his pillow. But I finally convinced him to look, and he was very impressed. He figured out very early on that I did it, so I've been the tooth fairy ever since. I remember that he told his classmates that the tooth fairy only *visits* their houses when they lose a tooth, but she *lives* at his house because it's his big sister."

Meredith's story is a testimony of how strongly we can bond with our half siblings, even if we get off to a rocky start. Some think that a large age difference between siblings automatically means that they won't be close, but that is not always true. As older half siblings, we may not enjoy learning that we'll have to share our parents, that our blended family has gotten another notch more complicated. But those worries fade away as we grow to love our new siblings, as we learn to care for them, play with them, and be good sisters and brothers in return. And sometimes we're not the ones who need winning over; Kara finds that her youngest half sibling managed to charm even their father. "My youngest sister, the five-year-old, is the only one who's not scared of my dad. He yells at her, and she's not intimidated; she laughs at him. He mellowed out so much after she was born, it is unbelievable. She is a free spirit, and she has a very loud voice, and she uses it all the time. I am so grateful for her in our lives."

The answer to the quiz question is C. As new older siblings, we need to feel important and trusted. If we feel like we no longer get any attention ourselves, we will resent the new baby. But if instead we are assured of our place in the family, we can enjoy our new little brothers and sisters.

Can I Have My Own Room?

▼ ▼ ▼ ▼ ▼ ▼ ▼ ▼ ▼ ▼ ▼ ▼ ▼ ▼ ▼ ▼ ▼ ▼

Quiz Question

Moving is:
   a. Completely traumatizing for any child under the age of eighteen
   b. Stressful, but tolerable to children if they are reminded that their families care about how they feel
   c. Fun
   d. Only a good idea if you have a big truck

▼ ▼ ▼ ▼ ▼ ▼ ▼ ▼ ▼ ▼ ▼ ▼ ▼ ▼ ▼ ▼ ▼ ▼

(Answer to quiz at end of section)

Children from blended families are constantly on the move, because we have so many people to visit and more than one home to be part of. What makes our rootlessness even more real to us is when our parents move one of our home bases entirely. When our parents get married, they usually want to live with their spouses. This means that one of the first activities we engage in as a blended family is rearranging our homes. For many of us, that means moving to a new house altogether, and for others, it means making room for a new person in the house we live in already. Most children move at some time in their lives, but what makes our moves so striking is that they are not only a scenery shift, but a cast member change as well. How do we react to sharing our space? What happens when we move out of one family and into another one?

When stepparents move in after the wedding, it can feel like they just don't fit in, which is why many families find a new place to live altogether. It was necessary for Abigail to move out of her house when her mother remarried because her stepfather literally didn't fit into their old house! She remembers: "It was a small house. I really liked it. The rooms were little, and the ceilings were low. But my stepdad is very tall, and he didn't fit into any of it. So we moved, and now everything is fine. Actually, even if he had been short we would have had to move, since my mom was pregnant, and we didn't have enough rooms."

Ben remembers the way his stepfather moved in gradually: "It was sort of a process over time. Gradually, more and more of his stuff ended up at our house, and he was there a lot, but he still had his own apartment. For the most part, they did it that way because they were scared about how my sister would react. Once my sister moved out, he moved right in."

Moving in with a new family can be very trying on our nerves, especially if we are not used to sharing a room. A seemingly small thing like sharing a room can bring up very large issues for us about how our families have changed. Suzanne recalls that her brother, Lee, had to share a room with their stepbrother, Josh, which caused quite a bit of friction in the house. Suzanne remembers: "They argued. Josh went in the backyard, and he sat there for the longest time. Lee went out and sat at the bus stop. No one realized they were gone; we just realized the house was quiet. Finally my mom went into their room to look for Lee. She opened the door and called, but no one was in there. She went out walking to look for him. She found him at the bus stop and asked him what he was doing. He told her he was going back to our old neighborhood to stay with a friend or something. She told him he was waiting for a bus going the wrong way, and then she persuaded him to come back across the street. It was obvious that he and our stepbrother both needed their own space." Older children need privacy, and when there isn't enough space for them to have their own bedrooms, planning and compromise are the only way to get enough alone time. We need a corner to call our own, or at least the freedom to ask for some time by ourselves. Our homes change drastically when new people move into them, and we need time and room to adjust.

Not just our homes, but our living situation in general may change dramatically when we are living with a stepparent. Some of us, like Jordan, went from a small, inexpensive living space to a regular home because of the added income of our stepparent. Jordan remembered that before they moved in with his stepfather, the living situation was decidedly cramped. "My mother, sister, and I had this tiny little apartment with two closet-sized bedrooms in a student housing complex. My mom wanted my sister and me to have our own bedrooms, so for four years she slept on the floor. There wasn't a study room or anything, so she wrote all of her papers on a kitchen table and slept underneath it at night." For Stewart, his mother's remarriage meant both a new house and a new life. "I think with a new marriage you have a new everything. A whole new life started for me. I remember moving and liking it because there were tons of kids in our neighborhood. I had lots of friends to hang out with suddenly, and we had a blast. My brother and I shared a room in our old house, but when we moved up to where I live now, the house was big enough so that we had our own rooms and an extra guest bedroom. I remember that I was happy."

Many of us associate a change in lifestyle with the entrance of a stepparent in our lives. For us, Erica and Vanessa, the experience of moving in with our stepdad changed both our lives, but in a different way for each of us. Erica remembers, "I was happy about the move because I could walk or ride my bike to school, which I hadn't been able to do before. I could walk around the corner to the drugstore and buy an ice cream cone for fifteen cents. Every day on our way home from school, my friend and I bought mint-chip ice cream sandwiches. As an adolescent, I really enjoyed the freedom that the small neighborhood gave me." On the other hand, Vanessa has a slightly less idyllic story to tell: "I was so angry that we had to move away. I missed my friends a lot. In fact, for the first three years that we lived in our new town, my grandmother drove a van full of my old friends for over an hour to my new house for my birthday party. Even though I made friends easily in our new neighborhood, I blamed our stepdad for a long time for taking me away from my old life."

Denise remembers that when she and her mom moved in with her stepdad, she was not so happy at first. Many of us are resistant to moving at the beginning and, like Denise, must learn to enjoy our new homes and communities. She told us, "I complained about the area we were moving to; I complained about the house; I complained about everything, now that I remember. I had to change schools again. I wasn't happy about moving, but it wasn't an issue about moving in with my stepdad, and it actually turned out to be the best thing for us. I had my own room, finally. I had a lot of attention, and I really liked my stepdad from the beginning. I was happy not to be alone all the time. When they got married, my home life changed structurally in that people were home and I didn't live with my mom in a weird dark condominium. It was good."

Sometimes moving away from our stepfamilies can be just as difficult a transition as moving in with them. Derek remembers that moving away from his stepfather was a sad event for him, because he was not going to have the kind of father figure he had wanted. "One day when I was at my grandmother's house, my mom came over with my sister and told us that we needed to move right then and we were leaving the state. The situation was that the guy my mom married had been involved in drug trafficking, and he was addicted to prescription drugs. It's hard to be in a marriage with someone you can't trust, so we were leaving. We paid a couple of guys to help us move everything out. We just threw everything that we had into garbage bags and put them in the truck. I remember being really disappointed because this father hadn't worked out. Since I never really had a father, at about that age I started feeling a little separated from other kids because they had fathers and I did not. I was beginning to think, 'Oh, gee, this is going to be really neat. I'm going to have a dad. We're going to do the whole thing. I'm going to be in the Boy Scouts like all the other kids. It will be great. We'll play baseball or something.' I never had that kind of thing." Leaving the home, and even the state, that his stepfamily lived in was difficult, but in the long run Derek thinks that it was "the best thing" for his family. He understands that his mother chose to leave because she feared for her family's safety, not because she wanted to deprive him of a father–son relationship. We need to understand and respect why our parents decide to move so that we can be willing participants in the transition. Children who are forced to move without a full explanation go through a considerably more grueling adjustment process than those who are aware of why their situation is changing.

Sometimes moving, for children of blended families, means relocating from the home of one parent to that of the other, permanently. "Moving from Mom's to Dad's" means actually changing our home base and making the other house a satellite, a place we visit but do not really call "home." This is different from the constant running back and forth between homes that many of us experience, because it implies that we live full-time at one house and only visit the other occasionally. It is a sticky situation to be in, because no matter what we do, we look like we are playing favorites with one parent and not the other. Important for parents to remember is the fact that just because we can live more easily with one parent does not mean that we love our other parent less. Living with people takes a certain level of compatibility that we may not have with one or another of our parents. We may not have it with either. This does not mean that we do not care about them, but it can make being part of their households uncomfortable for us. Alex decided to move from his father's to his mother's house when he was in sixth grade, and his father wanted some reassurance that he wasn't losing his son altogether. "I decided at the end of sixth grade that I was going to move down to my mom's. I decided pretty suddenly. It was late July, and my mom had been saying, 'Please move down here.' What else would you do if you were seeing your sons once a month? My dad's really into contracts, and when I said I wanted to live with my mom, I had to sign a contract with him that said I would come back for high school. I've signed so many contracts it is ridiculous. It's a really big deal to my dad that I get my Eagle Scout, so part of the contract was that I would keep going to Boy Scout meetings in a troop down in southern California, and that I would get my life badge by a certain time on a certain date. Another part of the contract was that I would visit a certain amount of time on a regular basis. It didn't surprise me at all that he wanted some reassurance like that." Understandably, our parents don't want us to leave the nest before they are ready to say good-bye. Sometimes we forget that which home we live in affects them, too. Alex's father, by requesting a written agreement that guaranteed he would not lose his son, acted upon the inclination that most parents feel. A written contract with our parents is probably too extreme for most of us. Nonetheless, it is important for parents to express their desire for their children to live with them. The catch is that parents must also stay sensitive to what their children want.

Moving out of one home or away from one part of our family is a big step to take for a child. When our parents have joint custody or an arrangement that allows us to see both of them often, they necessarily agree to live near each other. Many parents do not have this agreement, however, and when one decides to move away, it affects the other, because of us. We are the link between two homes that are otherwise deliberately unrelated. We are sometimes the only people who know what both of our parents are doing and what their plans are.

Laura felt especially uncomfortable in her middle position when her mother decided that they would move across the country, leaving the father Laura visited behind. What she eventually found was that moving away from her father's family in fact helped her grow up. "It actually was a lot better because I spent a lot of time at my mom's alone coming into myself. When I would go to visit my dad, I was older, and I had a sense of who I was. I had the opportunity for my personality to form in a way that I wouldn't have had if I'd lived right there, under everybody's expectations. The initial visit home after we had moved was stressful, and everybody made a big deal about it. My dad's extended family all thought, 'Oh, God. She's going to turn into her mom.' That was really everybody's fear. As soon as I came home they realized, 'She's taken care of; she's well adjusted; it's all okay,' and everybody relaxed about it. As soon as everybody saw that I was okay, it was more fun than it had ever been. The time we spent together was quality, and there wasn't so much chaos as far as shifting back and forth. Moving away turned out to be the best thing." This is not to suggest that all custodial parents should sweep their children away from their other parent; far from it. What this story really illustrates is the same point that underlies all our stories: We can survive large changes, we are able to grow up well even in chaotic living situations, and as long as we know our families love us, the transitions are usually tolerable.

The answer to the quiz question is B. Moving is stressful, but we can survive it if we know that we are still valued by our families. When moving in between our parents' homes, we need to be freed from the assumption that we love one parent more than the other.

Part Two

Living in Limbo

Everyone sees a bit of what it's like to live in a blended family. We all see kids shuffle back and forth from one parent's house to the other; we all hear answering machine messages that list four people with four last names. But what is it really like? How does it feel to be in the middle of all that? To learn to fly across the country alone at age four? To always be letting your friends know which house they should call to find you? To see your parent fall in love—or get dumped? To be mistaken for your baby half sister's mother—when you are only twelve? Not even the parents in a blended family know the answers to those questions. Even more important, no one knows how such experiences shape us in the long run. Parents are naturally interested in how childhood experiences will affect their children ultimately as adults. What will they remember forever, what will they laugh at, what will they forget, what were they really thinking? Here are our answers.

Living in a blended family exposes us to the fine art of compromise very early on. We try to be part of new families without breaking the ties that bind us to our other parent. We learn how to behave in two very different environments, both of which we call "home." Those of us who live with one parent and only visit the other struggle to feel comfortable in an unfamiliar home. We learn to balance our loyalties, and we try not to take sides. We become experts at mediating conflicts between our parents, who sometimes act like the children in the family. (Yet, like all good kids, we also figure out how to antagonize our parents, push their buttons, and extort money from them.) We find ourselves trying to explain our families to the world around us. Some incredulous friends think that we are strange, some supportive ones can empathize, and some teachers don't understand, no matter how many times we explain, who has signed our permission slip because the last name is unfamiliar.

Every child has a unique relationship with his or her stepparent. Traditionally, there is no preprogrammed role in a child's life for a stepparent as there is for a mother or a father. We all have different connections with our stepparents depending upon how old we are when they enter our lives, what our relationships with our biological parents are like, and what we, as individual children, are ready for. For a young child whose mother has passed away, a stepmother can be a welcome maternal presence with all of the authority and responsibility of a biological mother. Yet for an teenager who has a close relationship with her mother, a stepmom may be a friend, not an authority figure. Whether they become parental figures, older friends, allies, or enemies, stepparents are always a presence that affects our lives. Most of us are not cursed with an evil stepmother of fairy tale proportions. Our dramas are real, as are our celebrations.

We may spend half of our time in each home, but emotionally we are full-time members of both. Just as in any other family, in a blended family there are fights over the bathroom and romps through the house with cousins. We laugh at parties and grow closer in tragedies. We also have the singular experience of integrating another entire family tree into the equation, sometimes two or three. We are not part of just one, nuclear family, and that means that we live in limbo, in a constantly fluctuating mix of houses, people, affections, and bonds. So this is about the everyday occurrences in our lives. It is a discussion of the day-to-day struggles and triumphs that spring up in our blended families and how we learn to handle them.

Under New Management

▼ ▼ ▼ ▼ ▼ ▼ ▼ ▼ ▼ ▼ ▼ ▼ ▼ ▼ ▼ ▼ ▼

Quiz Question

When you move into a home with your new spouse and stepchildren, the first thing you should do is:

a. Throw away their TV and rearrange their bedrooms

b. Stand very still against a wall and tell them, "I don't want to get in the way"
c. Do your best to pit the children's parent against them. Then they will know who's boss
d. Blend in slowly, these transitions take time

▼ ▼ ▼ ▼ ▼ ▼ ▼ ▼ ▼ ▼ ▼ ▼ ▼ ▼ ▼ ▼ ▼ ▼

(Answer to quiz at end of section)

Once our parents remarry, we confront the changes their spouses make to our households. Not surprisingly, those changes range from small alterations in the house decor to enormous differences in the way we relate to our parents. How do we feel about those shifts? Although our reactions are as diverse as our circumstances, one trend is clear. We care about what happens to our families, and we are acutely aware of how they are different when a stepparent enters the picture. We are greatly affected by the amount of authority a stepparent assumes and by the way he or she changes our connections with our parents. We are particularly sensitive to how we fit into the new configuration.

For many of us, the new partnership makes us feel like a third wheel at first, especially when our old routines get shaken up because of the relationship between our parent and stepparent. Margarita, who moved away from home when she was seventeen, remembers what it was like to be around when her mother had just started her new relationship. "I think there's a way, when parents get divorced and before they start seeing anyone else, that their children become more precious to them than they were before. When parents first get divorced they try to make it easy for their kids. For some reason I think of a stereotype that says, 'If you're white and middle class and your parents get divorced, you're going to Disneyland.' That all changes when they find someone new. There is a shift in attention, and it made me feel somewhat out of place at home. My mom and her partner had new rules and a new religion, which made it much more difficult for me to feel comfortable."

While Margarita's feelings of displacement are common, she also had the unusual experience of watching her mother start a new partnership with another woman. Margarita says of her mother's partner, "Lynn and I get along together really well. I'm not sure if the traditional parent model is applicable to either my mom or Lynn anymore, although Lynn is family. There weren't any issues for me about the fact that my mom was involved with a woman. My brother got upset about it for a little while, but now they get along very well. He has written essays for school about how great it is to have a lesbian mom."

In a new household, old relationships will get redefined. Often we are afraid we will lose the closeness we had with our parents when they were single. Allison struggled to maintain a close relationship with her father after her stepmother entered their lives, and she describes how it felt: "My dad and I had an intense, very close, 'buddy' relationship. My stepmom is a counselor, and she influenced my dad by telling him that it wasn't healthy for him and me to be friends because I needed him to be a parent. She thought she was doing what was best for me, but after that, my relationship with my dad started changing a lot. She has always been very involved in my relationship with him, and it has been one of our stumbling blocks because you can't have a three-way relationship."

When Allison felt that her stepmother was becoming too intrusive, she looked to her father for support. "My stepmom and I had a couple of direct confrontations when I was living there. Dad was the one who had to decide who was right, and it felt like he was choosing between us. I had been my dad's best friend. I was his confidant; we shared everything; we laughed about everything. But inevitably, in every square-off that we had, Maria was the clear-cut winner. It might have been that he was just trying to do his job as a parent, but to me it definitely came down to who won and who lost. A lot of my relationship with my dad has been influenced by the fact that I felt that he had made his choice, and I felt that he had chosen against me." The relationship between husband and wife is entirely unlike that between parent and child. It doesn't seem logical for us to feel competitive toward stepparents, but if they receive the attention and loyalty we are used to having from our parents, we can feel hurt and betrayed.

There are other reasons why we struggle with stepparents, and sometimes it is as simple as apples and oranges: they just may not be people we would get along with anyway. Derek, who was raised primarily by his grandparents, felt that he had lost his father figure when his grandfather passed away. His grandmother remarried, and his step-grandfather is not someone for whom Derek has ever developed affection. He told us, "I didn't get along with the man my grandmother married. I still don't get along with him. I was in seventh grade when my grandmother began the relationship, and we would get into fights all the time. He would say things like, 'Oh, that boy should be working. He should be supporting his mother. He should be out on the farm by now.' Even as I've gone through school and done very well, his attitude has not changed. I remember when I told him I was an intern for our senator. His reaction ran along the lines of, 'How much money are you making doing that? You should be out picking berries.' Still to this day, he believes that because my mom is not married, I should be supporting her and doing the 'things that boys should do.' He just can't understand my life because it's so unlike his." Derek knew that his grandmother was happier because of her marriage, but he still could not connect with his stepgrandfather. Stepparents need to respect their stepchildren's personalities and life choices, and remember to offer advice or guidance only when it is invited. Derek would have felt closer to his step-grandfather if his stepgrandfather had been able to respect their differences. No one likes to feel their parents pressuring them to fit a mold, and it is especially angering for us to feel that our stepparents are coming into our lives with an agenda for us.

Seth had that experience with his stepmother. They are very different people, and she put a strain on their relationship by trying to influence him to become more like her. He told us that soon after he met her, "She started trying to be powerful. She didn't agree with the way my mother was raising me. The only way she could enforce the way she wanted me to be raised was through letters or phone calls, so the letters that I got from her were very vicious at times. The only time I ever talked to Anna was when she was trying to get me to change. That was hard." Anna broke the number one guideline for healthy blended family relationships: respect. How could she have behaved differently? She could have tried to understand who Seth was before she tried to "fix" him.

What happens when we can't get along with our step-parent? For Mark, the solution was simple: absence. He remembers that when his father remarried a woman he couldn't connect with, he visited his father less and less. "He got married, and that meant that when I would go to visit I would see him and his family. When I got a car I spent less time with him because I'd have to see his family, too." Mark had the luxury of being a little older and having his own source of transportation, but many of us are young and homebound. When times get tough with our families, we don't have the option of leaving when we feel like it or of deciding how often to visit. It then becomes essential to resolve the day-to-day struggles, one by one.

Meredith told us how those skirmishes played out for her. When her stepmom became part of the family, Meredith really felt as if the house was under new management. Her stepmother had a large amount of power, but both of them are quite headstrong, as exemplified by Meredith's version of the "Battle of the Chairs." She explained, "I had the infamous Battle of the Chairs with my stepmom. My sister and I never had good desk chairs in our room when we were little. We'd been without chairs entirely for a year when the battle started. We were getting older, and it was hard for us to do our homework at our desks because we had to crouch on our knees. We weren't supposed to work at the kitchen table because we would spread our papers all over the place, which annoyed my stepmom. Finally, she went out and bought us chairs. She got us the cheapest folding chairs she could find. As soon as I saw these things I knew they were already at death's door. She told me she didn't want to get me a nice chair because she didn't think I'd take care of it. We were supposed to use them every single day to sit on to do our homework, and they disintegrated. I took meticulous care of my chair because I knew trouble was coming. My chair still died. I was back to not having a chair. Then she told me that the real reason she didn't buy us nice chairs is because we couldn't afford them. Now, that alone doesn't have all that much significance, except for the fact that it was new bathing suit season. Somehow, in this planet where my sister and I cannot have chairs that work for more than a month, Evelyn managed to fit in a brand-name bathing suit for herself. She spent about seventy-five dollars on it. I've been to thrift stores where they have chairs that have been around since the dawn of time for ten bucks. I know she is just human but that was not a high point in our relationship for me." We understand why Meredith was so offended. One of the worst nightmares for a stepchild is the thought that their stepparent is going to take charge, control everything, and make changes that leave them feeling powerless and out of place. Evelyn's behavior which may have been simply a mistake or oversight felt like a direct attack to Meredith because it reinforced the fear that once a stepparent enters the family, the children are second-class citizens.

A stepparent may make many changes in a household, but our parents don't disappear. They are still the primary authority figures for us, and often they become the final mediators in sticky situations between their children and their spouses. Jordan remembers that his mother always had the last say when the issue involved him or his sister. "My stepfather wanted to be much more of a parental figure, and he wanted a lot more respect from us. I remember once he wanted to go to the hot springs. My mom and I had no problem with it, but my sister got very upset. She was crying, and she didn't want to go. Paul was getting angry with her, but my mom told him that if my sister wasn't comfortable, we weren't going. Period. So we all got in the car and went home." Like Jordan's mother, often our parents make a large effort to remind us that we are a priority and that what we think and feel does matter to them. They help us to feel safe asking for what we need and expressing our opinions. That kind of reassurance is invaluable to us when the family setup is shifting.

Figuring out how much power a stepparent will have is tricky, and there is no simple formula. Sometimes the lack of definitive roles is an obstacle because each person has a different idea of what a good balance of power looks like and different expectations for their families. After being divorced for several years, Greg's parents remarried each other. Even though his mom's new husband was his own father, Greg sounded like many of our other interviewees who experienced the entrance of a stepparent. He told us, "There was suddenly someone else making claims on authority, someone who could tell me what to do. I wanted to get to know him, and I wanted to make him 'Dad,' but I wasn't in the habit of it. He wanted me to do things like feed the pets and do housework and be more a part of the family. When it was just me and my mom, I did my own thing. I was an only child, so she let me have my world all to myself, and she didn't make too many claims on my time. But he wanted a conscious effort on my part to spend time with the family. I don't think he really understood that it was a big adjustment for me. He would take it personally if I did something he didn't like. The thing is, he hadn't caught me early enough to really shape my values as a young kid, so it came hard for me. He had to really fight me to do it, and I had to try really hard to want to do it." Even though it was sometimes an uphill climb, Greg feels that he was able to build a lasting relationship with his father. He told us that ultimately, "He earned my respect by treating me with respect." The work it takes to create and maintain healthy family ties is worth it.

Not all children have a difficult time transitioning into a blended family. Sometimes the benefits of having that extra person around are so big that the adjustments come easily. Being a single parent is never easy, and Hazel was glad when her dad didn't have to do it anymore. She says, "I don't think my dad and stepmom would have gotten married as soon if I hadn't moved in with him when I was young. I think he got the feeling that being a single father was too much for him. I remember one time when I was about twelve and I asked him to put my hair in a ponytail. His hands literally started shaking; he couldn't do it. He fiddled with my hair for an obscene amount of time, and by the time he was done, my hair was all tangled. My poor dad. I think the whole idea of having a daughter without an older female influence around scared him. He was much more open to marriage because of that." Luckily his plan worked, and Hazel is quick to extol the positive influence her stepmother had on their home. "She decorated the place so that it looked really nice; she made it more homey. We would stay up and talk, she would lend me her things, she would give me old makeup. It was like living with a friend. She is really a great person. My dad was relieved." Not all stepparents have to ease their way in slowly. What made Hazel's relationship with her stepmother work out, though, was the sensitivity her stepmother showed for Hazel's needs.

Seth's stepmother made enormous changes in his life that are especially precious to him. He had no relationship with his father at all until his stepmother came into the picture when he was in elementary school. He said of her, "That woman has done a lot for me. She brought my dad back to me. I owe her the world. When I was two years old, she basically told my father that if he wanted to continue a romantic relationship with her he would have to start seeing his son. My dad was scared and waited a while to do it, but he was willing to make a sacrifice because he loved her, and he wanted to see me. He found out what it means to be a father because of his new wife."

There are various means by which a stepparent can become part of our lives, and not all of them are revolutionary. For Suzanne, the changes in the household when her stepfather moved in were minimal, which was fine with her. She said, "It wasn't a big deal. People would come over and I'd say, 'Oh, that's Craig. Don't worry about him. He's just hanging out.' He didn't get in my way or interfere with what I was doing. He just wanted to do his thing; he wanted to work and make sure the kids were okay. He wanted to make us happy." Whether they made changes to the family or not, Seth and Suzanne's stepparents both showed that their motives were unselfish. They wanted to do what was right for the whole family, which is one of the best ways to earn a child's respect.

Even when stepparents enter quietly, everyone's habits change, and our lives are rearranged. We notice the small ways our stepparents influence our daily routines, even the appearance of the house. There are more toothbrushes in the bathroom and more dinner plates on the table. Jay was characteristically succinct when describing the differences after his stepmother moved into the house he shared with his father and brother. "Someone unfamiliar was living there, and I had to share my space with her. I remember it being strange that I couldn't walk around in my boxers anymore." He remembers that when his stepmother moved in, his house put on a new face: "We were three guys, two teenagers and a father, living together. It was dirty. Michelle moved in, and she was motivated to clean it. She brought a lot more income into the family, so one of the first things to happen was that we got a housecleaning service once a month. It really helped. It continues to help." Mark had a similar experience with his stepmother, but for him, the new home appearance seemed unnecessary. He remembers when his first stepmother entered the picture: "She had a lot of money. My mom works part-time and the house we lived in was a shack. I had lived there all of my life; the paint was chipping, and it was very dirty. I'd go over to my dad's place, and it was a totally different world. It was really weird. When he was married to my first stepmother he lived in a big mansion. You couldn't sit down on the couch, and you had to take off your shoes before coming in. My dad's not like that at all, and I don't know how he put up with my stepmother's expensive tastes."

Serena recounted that her stepfather made changes to their house that were welcomed by the kids, but not by her mom! "My mom was anti-technology, so we didn't have call waiting because she thought it was rude; we didn't have cable; we didn't have a house alarm. But my stepdad is totally normal about these things, so they are adjusting the rules. She always said that she would never let my brother have a TV in his room. I swear that after she got married, it was not three months before he had a TV, with cable. I remember when I lived there and my mom was the only parent, all those rules were totally inflexible. Now my stepdad is there, and everything is changing. My mom always had this old, decrepit answering machine that only sometimes worked. My stepdad is an attorney, and he needs to actually hear his messages, so he got voicemail. Three days ago I called, and they had just gotten it hooked up. I left this message for them: 'I am feeling betrayed. I am feeling marginalized. I am feeling unimportant; I told you you needed this for eight years and you never listened.' It was really funny. I told her that her outgoing message should say, 'Serena was right all along; leave a message after the beep.'"

But the changes didn't stop with electronics, as Serena discovered. "He's from Texas, and she's been living in L.A. for so long that there are a lot of things they have to teach each other. He is learning to respect cars, and she is learning to respect barbecue. She has new interests because of him. I came home for a visit, and she was bird-watching, something she had never done before. She looked at me with a straight face and said, 'They're amazing waterfowl!' When they got married, I was not only meeting a new stepdad, I was also meeting a new mom because I was seeing who she was in relation to him."

When we see that stepparents improve our parent's lives, they improve our lives as well. Zoe recalled little details that clued her into the fact that her mother was much happier with her stepfather. "This is pretty silly, but my stepfather and my mother kiss. I never saw my mother and father passionately kiss. Once while we were watching a movie, I turned around, and my stepfather was kissing her. I was about twelve, and it was the first time I had ever seen my mother be kissed!" Zoe told us that her mother and father both became better parents after they were remarried, because they were happier people. Lawrence had a similar observation about his own family. He was already a teenager when the largest changes in his family took place, and he recalled that his father's remarriage made his father a happier person, even though it shook up their family quite a bit. He said of his father, "He was pretty angry for a long time at the fact that his relationship with my mom wasn't working out. He used to get angry and frustrated at us kids when they were married, and he stopped doing that after he married my stepmother. His remarriage didn't affect my relationship with him negatively at all. My mom thought that was strange, especially after I learned that he had had an affair with my stepmom while he was still married to my mother. My mom asked me about whether the affair had affected my relationship with him. But it never did. In some ways he became a nicer person."

Lawrence's mother remarried after he had been at college for a few years. His description of how he felt is music to any parent or stepparent's ears: "My mother and I are really quite close. We don't spend as much time alone together now that she is married, which I miss, but her husband is great. He's very kind. And by the time it happened I was old enough that I didn't have any emotional problems or struggles with their marriage. My siblings and I were aware that she was lonely. We were all very happy for her."

It is difficult to predict how any child will react to the ways their stepparent changes the family, because there are so many kinds of stepparents and so many kinds of families. But in some ways, people are all the same. When we feel listened to, we will say how we feel. When we feel bossed around unjustly, we will usually resist. It is important for us to know that just because someone new has entered the picture, we have not lost our place in the family or in our parent's lives. We get along beautifully with stepparents who are sensitive to the fact that it is an enormous adjustment for us to accept them into our homes.

The answer to the quiz question is D. If there are any questions, please stay after class.

On the Road Again

▼ ▼ ▼ ▼ ▼ ▼ ▼ ▼ ▼ ▼ ▼ ▼ ▼ ▼ ▼ ▼ ▼ ▼ ▼

Quiz Question

When planning when and where your children will be, it is best to consult your ex-spouse:

    a. Not at all; in fact, throw away their phone number

    b. Regularly, so that the transitions go smoothly for the kids

    c. Only through lawyers

    d. Only through the kids

▼ ▼ ▼ ▼ ▼ ▼ ▼ ▼ ▼ ▼ ▼ ▼ ▼ ▼ ▼ ▼ ▼ ▼

(Answer to quiz at end of section)

"Are your bags packed?"

When we hear that signal, we know the traveling routine is about to begin. Most children of divorced families travel back and forth to see their parents, but we all have different schedules depending upon how far away our parents live, how old we are, what kind of custody arrangement has been worked out, which home we feel more comfortable in, and, of course, which one we think has more loopholes in the rules. When a parent remarries and a stepparent, stepsiblings, or half siblings are thrown into the mix, the seemingly simple traveling routine can dredge up many charged feelings for everyone involved. We often feel rootless as we travel back and forth between two homes and two families.

Those on the permanent ends have to deal with constantly losing and then regaining part of their family. This is usually hard for our parents, who are never satisfied with the reduced amount of time we spend with each of them. Relationships require time, and the only way for us to get any time with our families is to shuffle back and forth. The fact that our parents keep asking us to travel between their homes shows us that they value their time with us. Now we explore the different effects our traveling habits had on us. Most of us find that the actual travel may be difficult, but it does send us the clear message that our families care about us and want to be with us. That is precious knowledge.

For us, Erica and Vanessa, the routine was regular and predictable, but it took a great deal of careful planning. We saw our parents sit down together for a scheduling meeting every month. They realized that the only way we could grow up with two parents, and they could each have two daughters, was to cooperate. These scheduling meetings were friendly, perhaps not fun, but we learned that there would always be someone to take care of us. Erica remembers, "After our mom and stepdad moved an hour south, most of our meetings took place in the restaurant of a hotel that was our halfway meeting spot. Everyone would pull out their calendars and pens, except for Vanessa, who would be too busy eating wontons. I remember one day I decided I wanted to choose what time I would be picked up, and to their credit, my parents indulged my need for a little control. They said, 'Okay, Erica, will it be two, two-thirty, or three?' It sounds a little silly now, but at the time it helped me feel like an important contributor instead of just a bit of baggage to be transported."

Hazel also remembered that her parents split up the traveling responsibilities equally, and she joked with us about feeling like "baggage" herself. "My dad would usually just pick me up at my mom's house on the weekends. Finally, my mom and dad started working out this system of meeting halfway. My dad would drive exactly 10.5 miles, and so would my mom. We would meet at a hotel that was right off the freeway. It was kind of like a drug deal."

Usually when our parents live far away from each other, we can count on living with one family during the school year and spending the summers with the other. This setup works well for some children, like Rebecca, but she talks about why it was difficult to see her father only in the summer. "It was nice to spend a lot of time with him in the summer, because I think you get a much deeper relationship when you have everyday life with somebody. We had to get to know each other again every summer because I was changing a lot and he was trying to keep up, and that was the hard part about it. I think he put a lot of effort into it, and I am really glad he did. Especially when I started to become an adolescent, I think it was confusing for him because I would change completely from year to year. That was a pain for us both sometimes. But you do it; you do what you have to do." Rebecca trusted that her family would do their best to work together so that she could be part of both households. That trust is invaluable to children from blended families, and it is a trust that is not always easy to maintain.

For a lot of kids, having two homes provides an opportunity for one parent to ship them off when they get too difficult to deal with. Margarita's parents did not work to keep in contact, so for Margarita, going back and forth usually meant she was in trouble. She told us, "My mom kept kicking me out of her house. I'd go to my dad's house, and I couldn't really deal with my dad's house very well. I think that was the worse thing with their divorce. I already felt unsettled, and they kept shifting me around."

Sometimes the scenario reverses, and what happens is that when we get in trouble, *we* leave one turbulent household for a safe haven in the other! Often Laura would use having two disconnected homes to her advantage. She could always find refuge somewhere, because her parents both welcomed her in. "Anytime I would get in trouble, I always wanted a sane place to go to. If I was in trouble in one place, I didn't want the other person to know. When I was seventeen, the first time that I had sex, I told my mom. She totally flipped out. It was awful. I mean it was *awful*. I went to visit my dad's family, and I wasn't going to tell anybody because I just wanted to be there without a fuss. My freshman year in college I failed a class. I told my mom, but I wasn't going to tell my dad. I didn't want him to know."

Having an alternate home to go to when we need a break from the one we usually live in can be a healthy, rejuvenating experience. Tanya is nineteen and hopes to become a journalist. She remembers that when she was having a difficult time living with her mother, she could escape to her father's for a while, and it would cheer her up. She said, "One day when I was eight and a half, my mom and I had started fighting a lot, and I threatened to write to my dad and move in with him. I had a temper tantrum, and my mom called my dad and asked him if I could come visit him because I was so unhappy where I was. So that summer my dad drove all the way over from Arizona, about a sixteen-hour drive. He picked me up at 7:30 in the morning, we drove all the way back to Arizona, and I met my new stepmother and my new infant half brother, who was a week old at the time. That was really, really good. Every time I've gone to my dad's house I've had an awesome time." Traveling back and forth can make us feel both rootless and cared about. The best is when we feel the latter more than the former, because we can adapt to the transience as long as we know we are loved. Parents can help tip the balance in a few ways. One, of course, is by reminding us that their care for us is the real reason why we go back and forth. Making the effort to see us, whether it is by driving a long distance, buying us a ticket, or meeting us at the gate, is an important gesture that helps us feel wanted.

The love we feel from our parents can sometimes translate into their disappointment when we are unable to spend all of our time with them. Abigail remembers the hassle associated with traveling between two homes, even though her parents lived in the same town. "It really irritated me. When I was little, it wasn't a big deal because I didn't have much stuff. I'd have a toy, maybe, but I could put that in a backpack easily. By the time I got to middle school, I had stuff that I wanted to have with me, like music. I had only one stereo, so I would have to take that back and forth with me if I ever wanted to listen to music. But that was difficult because all the trading of houses took place on school days. So if I wanted something to go with me, other than what I was wearing, I had to take it to school. I started being really hostile about the fact that I never had all of my stuff in one place. I was always going for either two days or five days, which was never really long enough to make a big deal out of packing, but that meant I never got to take anything I wanted with me. I started lobbying for switching off less often. My mom was resistant to the idea because she really didn't want to go for a whole week without seeing me. Eventually I moved out of my dad's house and stayed at my mom's all the time. But that was after two years of negotiations."

Abigail's parents warmed up to having their children decide when they wanted to visit, but Abigail jokingly took complete credit for their recent flexibility. "A couple of years ago my younger sister started staying for a month at a time at each house. The first child had to break through all the rules. She never would have been able to stay for a month at a time if it hadn't been for me." Many of our families have to experiment for a time, sometimes for years, before we find a system that works for us.

Sometimes it doesn't look like we use a system at all. Especially if our parents live close to each other, we may not organize our visits very well. However, that can be taxing for parents and children alike, especially if our parents are unable to communicate with each other. Meredith had a particularly unsettled childhood and still can't get a coherent story about the visiting schedule out of either her mom or dad. "For a while apparently my sister and I were supposed to switch off every year. That was the theoretical scenario in which we lived with one parent full-time and with the other one on weekends and then switched the next year. It never worked out that way. If I ask them to explain why, my parents both have a version that makes it sound like they were a bunny rabbit swimming in a pool, with a big shark named either Madeline or David, depending on who you are asking, chasing them around. Because of that, I really don't know what the situation was at the time. I could expect to see a new house from one of them about every two months. Somebody was always moving, so I didn't visit either of them on a fixed schedule." Meredith was able to remain flexible, even though having such a chaotic schedule was sometimes very difficult. She advised, "If you are going to make a schedule, stick to it."

When our parents split up and remarry late in our childhood, we can experience a more strained transition into a blended family. Rosa didn't run from her mom's to her dad's for long, because she was on her way out entirely, going to college. But she has vivid memories of her father's first apartment and how it felt for her to be there. "My dad moved into an apartment, and my mom stayed in the house. It was a raunchy little apartment, it was really weird, but I thought it was cool, because I had never moved before. I'd been born in the house that my mother still lives in. I thought it was interesting that I had this new place; it had a pool, and I'd never had a pool before. But I thought it was very strange, and my brother thought it was really strange, and we would just sit around and be quiet because we weren't very comfortable there. My parents had joint custody for a while, so we would spend one month with one of them, and then we'd pack up all our stuff and move to the other place. I just thought the whole thing was odd, and I was happy to be taking off to college."

Seth's story is a perfect example of both the importance of traveling back and forth and its disorienting effect on us. He remembers the end of his first visit with his father: "On my way to the bus station I wouldn't let go of my dad's leg, so he dragged me along, attached to his leg. We went into the bus, and we sat down. We were there for twenty minutes before the bus left, and he was just talking to me. I was eight years old, and I had just spent the most wonderful three weeks in my life to that point. I didn't want to go back home. He brought out a box. I opened it, and in it was a brand new fishing pole. He knew that out of all the things we had done together, I had liked fishing the most. He admitted that I probably wouldn't use it while I was at my mom's, but he said that I should bring it with me every single time I came to visit him. It was an insurance policy that I'd come up to see him again."

Having two homes sometimes makes us feel unsteady. The traveling routine is most difficult when our parents are unable to communicate civilly, when they try to ignore the fact that we have another family, and when we feel pressed for time everywhere we go. We are most comfortable when our divorced parents can respect our divided lives. We need them to be aware of our desire to spend time with both of our households. Most important, when we are travel weary and tired of being relocated, we need to be reminded that we are trekking from one home to the other because everyone loves us so much.

The answer to this question is B. Even for parents who don't get along at all, consulting each other about where and when to pick up children is vital. We should not bear that responsibility until we are old enough to choose when we want to visit. Parents who communicate only through lawyers or not at all put much greater strain on us because we feel like a liability.

Adjusting to Fit

▼ ▼ ▼ ▼ ▼ ▼ ▼ ▼ ▼ ▼ ▼ ▼ ▼ ▼ ▼ ▼ ▼

Quiz Question

Your children (or stepchildren) travel back and forth between two homes. When you go to pick them up at their other parent's house, you should:
  a. Pretend that they had never been gone, and act uninterested when they talk about what they had been doing
  b. Make comments about how irresponsible and disorganized their other parent is

c. Welcome them, and allow them some time to make the transition

d. Chat endlessly about all of the fun activities you did without them

▼ ▼ ▼ ▼ ▼ ▼ ▼ ▼ ▼ ▼ ▼ ▼ ▼ ▼ ▼ ▼ ▼ ▼

(Answer to quiz at end of section)

Children who periodically switch households are a trademark of a blended family. Because we live with two different family roles, house rules, and daily routines, we can't help but compare them. In order to conform to two sets of expectations, we must fully understand them both, and so their contrasts become obvious. Most people can understand this in theory, but unless they, too, were a child who had to shuffle around, they cannot imagine what it actually feels like to be a member of two separate families. We are not living double lives; we are living one life that includes two homes. We need our families to try to understand, not to pretend the other household doesn't exist.

More often than not, our two homes are completely different, and every time we go from one to the other we have to adjust. When parents are just divorced, that transition is between Mom and Dad, people from whom we know what to expect. But when our parents remarry, the transition from one home to another can become even more conspicuous to us, because we are no longer the center of attention in both homes. Margarita, who lives on her own, explained the difference in her mother's and her father's houses now that her mother has a new family.

"When I see my dad, he usually doesn't do anything else. When he's supposed to see me, we go to the beach or out to lunch or something. We sit around and talk. He will try to make a time to see me when he doesn't have my brother or sister there. Even though it's a house I never lived in, I feel comfortable at my dad's. Whenever I go to see my mom, they have eighty things to do that day. My one chance to talk to my mom is when we are grocery shopping, because otherwise her partner, Lynn, or the kids are around. It is understandable, because she does have a busy lifestyle. They have a really developed sense of home there, but it's not my home. At my mom's house there is no room for me, and I always feel like a guest. I don't live there, and I really feel out of place. I don't fit in with the new household she has."

For most of us, there were differences between our households before our stepparents entered them. However, we usually find that a stepparent makes already existing differences even more prominent. Nora used a metaphor to describe how different her two homes are. She told us, "It's as though I was going from the East Coast to the West Coast all the time. When I actually went to Boston for the first time I felt like I was surrounded by my father. Sometimes I cannot get people to believe that I'm from the West Coast, because I am so much like him." Seth's description of the main difference between his mother's and his father's is more extreme: "It's as if the Constitution really does hold true at my mom's house. But when I go to my dad and stepmom's house, it's China. I can't say whatever I want, like I can at my mom's. It's hard."

Mark also experienced a disturbing disparity between his two homes. He told us, "My mom worked three jobs when I was growing up, so I would be home a lot more than she would. Since just the two of us lived there, it was my house. I loved it. When I would go over to my dad's, everyone would be there: my dad and his wife and her sons, and I couldn't do anything. I had to take off my shoes, and I couldn't get snacks in between meals. I didn't do anything in the house. I went to my room, which was also the guest room, and waited until I could go home."

Nora, Seth, and Mark's stories hint at that ever-present problem in divided custody families: the "real parent" versus the "fun parent." Many kids live with one family while they are in school and going to bed on time, and the other family on weekends and during the summer. Parents end up in the awkward situation of playing only one role: nagging disciplinarian or fun-loving entertainer. Ben remembered that visiting his father was like going on vacation: "I lived most of the time in my mom's house. My mom was much more authoritative than my dad. When I came to my dad's house, it was like Candyland. He would give my sister and me money. He would give us a walkie-talkie, and we'd go roaming around town. Just in case anything happened, we could call back to the home base. We could do whatever we wanted."

The problem can get even worse when stepparents enter. As Abigail told us, "My mom was the fun parent, and so when she married my stepdad, he had to be the disciplinarian. That made my sister and me mad, because we didn't feel like he had that authority over us. It happened again when my dad married my stepmom. My dad had always been the serious parent and my stepmom was the fun one, so my stepbrother would get mad because he didn't want my dad to tell him what to do."

There isn't always a dichotomy between discipline and fun, and there shouldn't have to be. Vanessa remembers that she didn't understand when our mother complained about the lack of "fun time" she had with us. She says, "One time I remember Mom saying that she was disappointed in the way our schedule worked out because our dad got to have us on the weekends, when all of the fun stuff happened. I really hadn't thought of it that way until then. In fact, I was a little annoyed by it, because I thought she saw us all of the time and he saw us for only two days a week. It hadn't even occurred to me that the nature of the time we spent with her was any different, because it felt like we did have fun together. In that case, I felt fine about the setup but she felt like she was boxed into a role."

In divorced families there is a stereotype that the mom is the weekday, real parent, and the dad is the visiting, weekend, fun parent (just watch *Mrs. Doubtfire*). As is clear from Abigail's story and others, that stereotype doesn't have to be true. The best parents can be both. If the visitation schedule is at fault for making parents and stepparents play certain roles, that schedule can be changed. Some blended families deal with the problem by arranging for the kids to spend vacation time with both parents. (That's what our family learned to do.) Or, better yet from the kids' point of view, all the parents can become fun parents!

Most parents aren't as bad as the stereotypes, but they do have different standards. Adaptability becomes second nature to most of us, and we develop an acute understanding of what behavior is and is not acceptable in each of our families. Abigail playfully explained the unspoken rules about manners and sarcasm in each of her homes: "If my sister asked my dad what kind of pizza we were having for dinner, my dad would think it was funny to say, 'The really bad kind,' with a serious face, and that would be the end of the conversation. You would not find out what kind of food you were having, other than 'the really bad kind.' If my sister asked what was for dinner at my mom's house, my stepdad said, 'pizza,' and then I said, 'the really bad kind,' it was not funny at all. They thought I was insulting my stepfather's pizza."

When we are clear about what the rules are, we can easily go overboard in our efforts to behave. Denise remembers that all she wanted was to make sure that her parents weren't upset with her. "I was a really good kid; I was trying to please everybody. When you have a split family, this only comes out if you talk to other people, because how would your parents know? I'd be one way on the weekend and literally another way during the week because my parents had totally different expectations of me and I wanted them to both be happy. So I lied a lot, but I behaved. I lied about stupid stuff to keep them happy." Ideally, children would not feel so much pressure to conform that they would have to lie as often as Denise. Parents who understand that we are operating within two separate rule systems can help us by relieving the pressure to do it right all of the time.

Allison also had to behave differently depending upon where she was, because her parents had very different theories about discipline. She explained to us what that was like: "With my mom, if you do something wrong and you act like you are sorry and you make her laugh, you are okay. My sister and I used to play a game called Grapefruit Ball. All that means is that we'd get a big stick and smash the crap out of all these grapefruits that grow in the backyard and splatter them all over the place. We knew we weren't supposed to do it, but it was so fun. When our mom came home and found us, we'd make up a story about how aliens invaded and they blew up all these grapefruits and we had to fight them off. As long as we would clean it up and we could make her laugh, we were going to be all right. At Dad's house, I had no such luck. There was no slack whatsoever. Some people call it 'Control Freak.' Some people just call it 'Good Disciplinarian.' It just depends on who you talk to. He is very strict. If I had smashed grapefruits in his and my stepmom's backyard, I wouldn't have a story to tell about it. I'd be dead. The things that made my stepmom angry were not the same things that annoyed my dad, and neither of those were even vaguely like the things that made my mom angry. So I just had to remember who I was dealing with and what was going to make them mad. Everyone in my family will attest to the fact that I frequently forgot both."

When we forget which rules we are supposed to be following, we inevitably run into trouble. Margarita's mother and her partner run their home on a strict schedule. Margarita told us, "Their house is really their symbol of their new life. The house is a source of identity for my mom in the new role that she has, and I just don't fit in there. Unlike my dad, my mom gets really mad if you forget your chore or do it late. I learned not to stay there for more then one night so they couldn't get used to having me there and give me any chores. If you're new somewhere, you'll totally forget something that's not part of your routine. And then everyone gets really bothered that you forgot. I left some tools out in the backyard once, and my mom and Lynn were seriously mad. They told me they didn't want me to come back and visit them because I had messed up their house." Margarita's parents aren't mean people, they had just forgotten that Margarita was not used to living by their rules. Most of us have experienced a parent saying to us, "I don't care how you do it at your other house, that's not how we do things here." The real trick for us is to remember and respect which rules apply where, and the trick for parents is to be understanding when we forget. We all must be able to see the situation from the other's point of view, if we are to live in peace.

Usually we are able to navigate the different codes of conduct we encounter in our separate families. However, in addition to our occasional forgetting of which rules apply where, behaving differently in two homes can catch up with us in ways we don't foresee. Religion caused a problem for Laura when she tried to hold dissimilar standards at her two homes. "My mom was an atheist when I was young. When I would say, 'God,' she would say, 'What are you talking about?' We would celebrate Winter Solstice instead of Christmas. My dad and stepmom came from huge Catholic families, so on the weekends I would go to Sunday school. The week before I was supposed to make my first communion, my dad came into my mom's house with me when he was dropping me off and mentioned that I was going to make my first communion the following week. My mom didn't know that I had been going to Sunday school. She had no idea that it was happening because I didn't tell her. I knew that it would upset her. So we had a huge fight, and it got to the point where my mom started speaking for me, telling my dad that I didn't believe in God, and my dad was feeling bad for putting me in a position that he didn't know that he was putting me into. Eventually he just gave up and told her that because he didn't want me to lead a double life, he and my stepmother would just stop seeing me. There I was, seven-years-old, and I said, 'No, I want to see my dad every weekend so I'll make my first communion.' My mom let me do it, but she told me to cross my fingers." The compromises we make to be with our family sometimes seem endless.

We aren't the only ones who have to make compromises. Blended family parents have to make them, too. Laura's parents genuinely cared about her, but they weren't sensitive to her other responsibilities. Laura told us, "When your family gets fragmented, everybody has their own agendas going on. I was taken care of, but I was really stressed out all the time because I would say to my dad and stepmom, 'I need to be home at my mom's by six.' They always said they'd take care of it, but they didn't understand what it felt like to have a mom who was home waiting for me. It was really stressful."

We can adjust to being in one household for a time, but we do not forget the other one. It is common for us to feel that both of our families wish the other one didn't exist. This alienates us, because we rarely agree. Usually, we want to be part of both our parents' lives. We are not suggesting that parents and stepparents coordinate every detail of their households with those of their children's other family; that would be impossible! Many children successfully deal with growing up in two homes, but it is much easier when our parents are understanding about the adjustments we have to make. We make our transitions, and we learn two sets of ropes, because we would rather learn how to be members of two families than just visitors in either.

The answer to the quiz question is C. Parents need to be respectful of the fact that we are dividing our time between two families and to refrain from making us feel guilty for spending time with one and not the other. Sometimes it takes us a little while to get "back into the swing" of one family after being with the other.

You Can't Ground Me, You're Not My Mom!

▼ ▼ ▼ ▼ ▼ ▼ ▼ ▼ ▼ ▼ ▼ ▼ ▼ ▼ ▼ ▼ ▼ ▼

Quiz Question

You are a new stepmother, and you are worried about what your role is in your stepchildren's lives. The best way to find out is:

a. Try to make friends with them before you assume any authority
b. Order them around as much as you can. They'll rebel sometime, and then you'll know where to stop
c. Never speak to them directly, send all messages through their biological parent
d. Read *Cinderella*

▼ ▼ ▼ ▼ ▼ ▼ ▼ ▼ ▼ ▼ ▼ ▼ ▼ ▼ ▼ ▼ ▼ ▼

(Answer to quiz at end of section)

Everyone expects a parent to be a disciplinarian. It is part of the job, right? Not so for stepparents. They are not automatically handed executive privilege over all disciplinary procedures, like biological parents are. However, some stepparents still feel the need to exercise punitive control, and the plain fact is that they generally are met with youthful resistance and rebellion. If they begin asserting authority while we are still adjusting to the idea of another adult in our lives, we are bound to react. How much authority our stepparents have in our lives is easily the most difficult negotiation our blended families must face.

This is not to say that all stepparents must therefore fade into the background of our lives without a voice in our upbringing. On the contrary, most of us hear our stepparent's advice (or feel our stepparent's wrath) at one time or another. The key is that we must be ready to listen to them, and they must be willing to listen to us. The balance of power in a blended family is delicate, and compromise is usually our ticket to living together successfully.

We have many fears about our parents remarrying, and one of the classic scenarios involves a stepparent who enters a family with the idea that he or she will change all the rules and reorganize the entire disciplinary system. The dreaded plot also includes a parent who defers all authority to our stepparent, subjecting us children to new, cruel, and unusual punishments. Thankfully, that is not the case for most of us. Nevertheless, there is usually some bargaining, even clashing, between us and our stepparents as we try to figure out how much power they should exert in our lives. Nora remembers that she worked very hard to keep her stepfather from overstepping his bounds. She told us, "He has 'other' ideas about raising kids. His father was a police officer, a really strong disciplinarian. My mom was a hippie. My mom was really calm with me. My stepfather showed up and said, 'We need to get this one in line.' And he still says that I would be a horrible brat if he hadn't showed up. I'm not really sure that's true. He tried to get me to call him 'sir' at first. It lasted about three hours before I told him, 'I'm sorry. This is just not going to happen.' I constantly had to be very willful in order to force him back into a system that we could all deal with. I really didn't know what the system was, but I knew that if one force got too strong, then the whole family would get thrown out of whack. If he had too much control over me, then I'd be miserable, my mom would be miserable, and their relationship would be weird."

We can easily disagree with our stepparents about how much clout they will have when we are to be punished and whether or not they are allowed to direct us without our parent's involvement. Martin found that his stepmother tried to exert her influence over him immediately after the first time they met: "I was staying for a couple of weeks in the apartment where my dad was living with my stepmother. Basically he would go off to work, and it would just be me and my stepmother in this apartment by ourselves with nothing to do except talk to each other. This was of course a little bit uneasy. I was having trouble with math in school. She tried to teach me multiplication tables and stuff like that. And I was annoyed about that, as I had just gotten out of school, and I wanted to have my summer vacation. There was an issue that developed between us about her trying to force me to do math, and me not seeing her as an authority figure. I didn't want her to try to teach me or discipline me. I actually remember getting into a fight with her one night. I told her that she should stop trying to be my mother because she was not and would never be. After I stood up to her and told her I didn't like the way she treated me, she did not do that ever again." However, the tension between Martin's stepmother and his sister still continues. Martin explained: "There was one instance when my stepmother was yelling at my sister and trying to discipline her. My sister yelled back, and my stepmom tried to slap her. My sister ran out of the house and tried to run away. My dad grabbed her, trying to stop her, and she kicked him. My sister stopped talking to my dad because of it, until very recently. She still refuses to talk to my stepmother." Martin's stepmother's behavior destroyed the relationship between her and Martin's sister. Perhaps Martin's sister was no angel, but her childish behavior is understandable: she was a child. Many families struggle with issues of discipline and control, which can spark intensely angry disagreements. Most of us do not find ourselves in physical fights with our stepparents, but it is necessary to acknowledge the reality of blended family relationships that are painful and emotionally scarring. Telling these stories is important so that we can learn from one another's experiences and share one another's wisdom.

One very effective way to let stepparents know how we feel about their disciplinary attempts is to tell them. If we confront our stepparents directly about the fact that we do not see them as authority figures, usually they understand. Sometimes it takes more than one reminder, though. Lucy said that the only time she really had a problem with her stepfather was during disputes about authority. "My sister and I were big enough when our mom married our stepdad that he didn't really get to be the disciplinarian. The only time I remember being very hostile toward him was when he would try to make rules. I didn't feel he had any business doing that. If my mom told me to do something, I might fight with her, but I'd probably do it. But if he told me to do something, I would just say to myself, 'You don't get to make me do that,' and then I wouldn't do it. My mom would be caught in the middle because I was old enough to say, 'He doesn't get to do this; if you want me to do something, you tell me to do it.' She wanted him to feel like he was in the family, but she also didn't want me to feel that he was usurping the place of authority. He figured that out eventually, and things finally smoothed out." A stepparent's role in the family is ambiguous at first. Rather than waiting for all the loose ends to fall into place, families should help each other define the new balance of power, and then adjust to the arrangement. Lucy and her mother began by making their wishes clear, and were able to find an equilibrium eventually.

Lucy's experience with her stepmother didn't pan out quite as easily. Her stepmother did not communicate well with her about how the rules were going to change in their household, and Lucy felt that no matter what she did, she was doing something wrong. She described how her relationship with her stepmother began to deteriorate: "We had a two- or three-week fight, and it felt like no matter what I did for those two weeks, I got in really big trouble for it. I had never been required to ask permission to have friends come over. All of a sudden I had to, but nobody told me that. I just got in really big trouble when I didn't. Once I figured that out, I would ask, but I'd ask my dad's permission. On one occasion he failed to tell my stepmom about it, and I got in really big trouble again. She yelled and screamed at me and wanted to kick me out of the house, and I never really knew exactly what I had done wrong. She would tell me I should move to my mom's house and that she didn't know why I wanted to live with them anyway. My dad would never intervene. He would be in the room sometimes, and afterward he would try to calm us down, but he never said, 'Hey, stop it, you don't get to kick my daughter out of the house.' Eventually I got tired of it. The whole thing was ridiculous, and my dad was taking her side more often then not. It was a very weird, angry, unhappy several weeks. Finally I moved out of my dad's house and into my mom's house for good. I don't think I've been as close to my dad since that time. He and I get along fine now, although things are still a little touchy with my stepmom." Ideally, everyone, including stepparents, parents, and kids, would be included in discussing and deciding the house rules, so that no one is left in the dark.

Kara wasn't happy with the rule changes in her father's house because she moved in as an adult and didn't expect to be treated like a child. She was completing a graduate degree and living with her father and stepmother to keep her costs down. She told us, "Mine is a unique situation because the first time I really lived with them, I was already grown up. My stepmother and my father had told me that they weren't going to put me on the chore list because I was too old for it. Then three weeks later my stepmother got up early one morning and announced, loudly, that it was chore day. All of a sudden I was on the chore list, without discussion, because my stepmom said so. I just didn't come out of my room. I cleaned my room, but I wasn't leaving. When I finally opened my door, there was a little sign dangling from the door frame that said, 'These are your jobs.' I thought, 'How insulting.' It was hanging so that I would open the door and see it twirling in the wind. I couldn't believe it. My stepmother came up to me later and asked if I was angry at her. I looked at her. I said, 'No; I'm fine; are you mad at me?' Which was crap; I was angry. I was really peeved; I just wanted it to be over. She was mad at me and I was mad at her, and neither of us was admitting it; it was totally dysfunctional. I can look back on the situation and know that it wasn't healthy, but I was in a place where it wasn't safe to be who I am." Kara's story is a testament to how challenging it is to communicate honestly. Even when we know it is what we are supposed to do, we can take the easy way out by covering up how we feel and pretending that everything is just fine. Eventually, it is best to tell the truth about what makes us uncomfortable, especially with regard to discipline. That is the only way to find a system everyone can agree upon.

Lydia had to be very strong in order to keep her voice heard in the family. However, she had unusual circumstances. Her mom's live-in boyfriend was the disciplinarian in her life for many years, but he was abusive to both her and her mother. "My mom was lenient with me when I was little. She still is. He was the one to discipline me, or if I got in trouble, my mother would tell him what was happening, and my punishment was normally up to him. It didn't bother me so much when I was little. When I got older and started to have a brain of my own, I started to realize that some of the stuff he was doing wasn't cool, and I was vocal about it. I didn't keep it to myself; I got really loud and obnoxious. He owned several guns and he kept them in a gun rack in the front hallway. He also kept a gun loaded on his side of the bed, and he told my mom that if she wasn't careful she'd end up dead. That's the biggest lasting impression I have of him, trying to scare us. I remember fighting with him once, as in standing up to him and getting somewhere. I actually had to go over to the gun case; the case was never locked. I took out a gun and held it to his head and told him that if he didn't leave me and my mother alone I'd kill him, and I had no qualms about doing it. I was twelve years old, and I was holding a shotgun. I didn't think it was right. I knew it was completely wrong, but it was the only way I thought I could get his attention. And he left. That was it. I know that it's horrible." Most poignant in Lydia's awful story is her strength, her resilience, and her ability to see that the family she was in as a child was unhealthy. Today, she is clear and articulate about what her mother and this man did wrong, she understands exactly how it has affected her, and she is consciously modeling herself on a different standard than the one she was given. But not all children are able to do that, and none should have to. There are stepparents who treat their stepchildren abusively, and we believe that no parent should remain in a relationship with someone who treats their children disrespectfully, especially if they are violent. Children need protection, and ultimately it is the parents' job to protect and nurture their children, not put them in harm's way.

Our willingness to comply with a stepparent's rules is greatly affected by our relationship with our other parent. For example, if we have a long-standing, healthy relationship with our father, we are much more likely to resist the authority of our stepfather. Even if we have only a strong loyalty to a faint memory of our biological parent, we may resist our stepparent. We can easily perceive them as trying to take our biological parent's place in our lives, which is usually not what we need or want for them to do.

Telling a stepparent that they do not have power over us is one thing, but reminding them that they aren't our *real* parent is another. When we call attention to the fact that a stepparent is not actually related to us, we are creating distance. Maturing children often look for ways to assert their autonomy, and for those of us with stepparents, this is one salient way to say, 'I don't need a parent!' Usually this issue comes up in families where the stepparent performs many of the duties of a biological parent and does take on a measure of power in our lives. When stepparents don't play a parental role, we feel no need to remind them of the fact that they are not our actual mother or father, because they know it already. The problem is that we usually say the words, "You're not my *real* parent," when we are angry, in order to hurt our stepparents.

Stewart remembers that he and his brother used it as a trump card in a few heated arguments. Stewart's stepfather was really a parent to him, so he knew that reminding him of the fact that they weren't related by blood was very hurtful. He recalled, "There have always been times when my brother and I would just say, 'You aren't even my real father.' If we were angry, we would throw that in his face. Whenever he would criticize us we'd always say, 'What about your *real* children? *They* just borrow money from you!' We would rub salt in the wound. He didn't have a close relationship with them, and they took advantage of him. After we said it we'd bite our tongues, though. It was clearly said in rage; it was one of the things you say when you are mad at someone. Everybody knows the things that can push someone's buttons. Whenever we used that, we'd run out of the room because we'd think a bomb was going to go off or something." Parents and children both need to remember that what matters in a family is how we care for each other, not whether we are related by blood.

Authority and the right to parent are certainly some of the more confusing and potentially painful areas of our relationships with our stepparents, especially if the role they take in our lives is more like that of a biological parent than a friend. However, sometimes the very presence of a stepparent is enough to trigger our loyalty response, even if they aren't trying to be our "new mom." Jay's experience illustrates the potential for rebellion, even when a stepparent is trying to be reasonable. His stepmother didn't expressly try to be his new mother, but he remembers feeling resistant to her anyway at first. He told us, "We didn't get along very well at first because I had a real problem with saying, 'You're not my mother,' and that whole thing. We had a couple of problems, but the biggest one was that I was driving around in her car a lot, and I was being kind of a brat and wouldn't accept her as any kind of authority figure. If she did confront me, I gave her no respect at all. I think it was just because she was not my mother. She was another adult moving into my house and telling me what I should do with the car I was driving. I was really defensive because my parents didn't get along very well, and I was trying to make it clear that she was not going to replace my mother at all. She demanded some respect, of course, because I was driving around in her car. She should have been able to tell me what to do with it. She was clear about that. But I wasn't." To Jay's credit, he accepts the responsibility for these altercations.

One of the major factors that affects how much we accept our stepparents' authority is our age. When stepparents enter our lives during our young childhood, we are more apt to respect them as elders and as some form of parental figure. The more we age and the more independence we gain, the more likely we are to resist their disciplinary influence. When we are older, we are much more skilled at being friends with our stepparents, and we appreciate their respectful distance. We have a difficult time accepting them if they try to control our lives. Suzanne remembers that her stepmother did just that, and it is a primary reason why they are not close. When Suzanne went to visit her father and stepmother as a teenager, there were clashes over what she wore and, especially, who she could be friends with. "One time I went to visit a bunch of guys that I was friends with. I told my dad exactly where I was going. My stepmom decided that she didn't want me over there anymore, and she came busting in. She knocked on the door, and then she came in and told me that I had to leave because she didn't want me hanging out with those people. I was thinking, 'Excuse me? Wait a minute. Who are you to decide?' But I wasn't going to stand up to her. My dad was so wrapped around her little finger that he would have come in there, grabbed me by my ears, and said, 'Get out.' So I said, 'I'll leave with you, but give me five minutes. Let me say good-bye and be polite.' So I said good-bye, walked out the front door, and said, 'Do you know what? That was really rude. I finally have friends here that are my age, and you're flipping out.' She told me that I didn't need that many guys to be my friends and that I was setting a bad example. She was very worried about what other people thought of our family, and I did not fit in her plan. I was not the stepdaughter she wanted. I wasn't the perfect child. I didn't actually do anything bad, she just didn't like how I dressed and who I associated with."

Problems like these probably arise more because of adolescence and its effects on both parents and children than because of the step relationship. But those sparks can start big fires. Relationships between stepchildren and stepparents can get very tense during adolescence, and it is important to remember that adolescence doesn't last forever. A teenager is a teenager, and she needs the freedom to be herself.

Suzanne's stepfather knew that it was a bad idea to interfere directly with how she was raised, but he did want her home to be consistent. She remembers that he was noticeably soft-spoken about discipline, even though he tried once or twice to uphold her mother's rules. "My mom had grounded me from the TV. She forgot about it and invited me to come sit with her and my stepdad to watch television when they got home from work. Craig, my stepfather, looked at my mom and said, 'Didn't you just ground her from the TV?' I thought that was the funniest thing. He was really passive about it. He didn't show much emotion. He just quietly asked the question. It would have been so perfect because my mom would never have remembered. It was great, though. He always hesitated to take any part in disciplining me. I never was upset about it because it was so funny when he did say something."

Stepparents who make an effort to uphold our parent's rules usually do just fine by us. The problems arise when they try to make their own rules, because many of us won't abide by them. Jordan always felt that his stepfather's authority was conditional, and so he didn't feel inclined to recognize it. He had a vivid picture of what the power structure was like in his family, and he describes his stepfather's place: "He was allowed to discipline us, but there was always the understanding that the power didn't rest with Paul, it rested with my mom. He was granted some power on temporary status, but it could be revoked at any time. His big cause was that he always wanted us to do chores. He was a very hard worker. When I was a teenager he would say, 'Do the chores,' and I'd say, 'I don't want to do the chores,' and he'd say, 'Do the chores.' We would go back and forth like that. I'd go to my room. He'd come upstairs, yell at me more, and then say, 'You're grounded.' I'd go and talk to my mom and ask, 'Am I grounded?' But I almost never was. It was always like that, and I think that was very difficult for him." Jordan seems to have emerged unscathed (growing up helps); these interactions may affect our stepparents more than they do us!

For some of us, stepparents have just as much authority as our real parents, if not more. This is usually the case when our stepparent has been in our lives since our early childhood, performing many, if not all, of the parental tasks in partnership with our biological parent. Stewart, who was raised by his mother and stepfather, remembers that his mother performed only minor disciplinary actions. "The old tradition in my Italian family is punishment by spoon hitting. It wasn't like my mom hit me for actual physical punishment; it was more like she was saying, 'I am in control; you need to eat your green beans.'

She punished me for little things like that. When it came to larger issues, she played it really neutral. When my stepdad and I fought, usually she'd just try to calm us down. She'd try to play the mediator and not take sides. My stepfather was the real disciplinarian." Our battles with certain stepparents stem from the fact that our biological parents *do* listen to their discipline decisions. If they change the rules, and our parent agrees, we are forced to respect them. When we break them, it is an overt action against not only our stepparent, but our parent as well. Although less ambiguous, this situation can also be trying for us if the new rules are not to our liking.

Meredith remembers that when her stepmother moved in, the focus of their house changed entirely, and she was expected to follow a completely new set of rules: "I really love Evelyn a lot, and I think that she is a great person, but the one thing I don't like about her is that she is Princess of the Universe. Really, the new rule of our house was 'How can the world be most convenient and least annoying to Evelyn?' If something annoyed her, it was completely against the rules. When I was in junior high school, I had a habit of wearing safety pins in my pierced ears because I could never afford earrings, and because I would always manage to stab myself in the back of the head with those little posts they have. But when Evelyn was around, wearing safety pins in my ears was against the rules. It was not allowed. I was required to take them out before I walked in the house. There wasn't anything actually morally wrong with wearing safety pins,

Evelyn just didn't like how it looked, so it was against the rules. We often got in trouble for singing. If she was tired or something she would say, 'You need to stop singing or go to your room.' I got yelled at a lot for laughing too loud. Evelyn felt that my guffawing was excessive and my dad just backed her up on everything." No one likes being asked to observe arbitrary rules. We understand that some of the things we do are irritating to our parents and step-parents. Some of the things they do annoy us, too. The problem is that parents hold the power, and occasionally forget to be fair. When making rules, make sure to give your children a good reason to follow them. ("Because I said so" is not a good reason. "Because you might fall off of that and break your leg," is.)

Even for stepparents who have as much authority in our lives as biological ones, the game is not completely over. We are still going to challenge them, as we would any parent. Like Meredith, Allison illustrated the kind of struggle she went through with her stepmother, whose role in her life was largely parental: "Maria and I had had many conversations about my appearance. We'd had many battles, many heartfelt, crying conversations, and we had come to the agreement that I was a good kid, I wasn't doing drugs, I wasn't getting pregnant, I wasn't bombing cities or anything, and if I wanted to look like a weirdo, it was my body. If I wanted to shave my head, if I wanted to dye my hair blue, if I wanted to dress however I did, it was my look; it was my thing, and she respected that. I thought the matter was fully settled. One night I called to say, 'I am staying out a little bit longer, do you mind?' She said that she didn't and then asked what I was going to be doing. I told her, 'Oh, I'm going with a few friends to get our tongues pierced; I'm really excited. I've been wanting to do this for a long time.' Now the whole extended family was over that night, and Maria answered the phone in the living room, so everybody heard when she said, 'You're what? You're getting your tongue pierced?' Suddenly she just told me no, I couldn't do it. After all of her talk about letting me express myself, she became hypocritical. I feel that she acted that way because the whole family was there. Everybody was watching her, and they hadn't been there for all of our heartfelt conversations, when we decided that she was going to respect my personal and fashionable boundaries. So I was pretty angry, let me tell you, and I went out and got it pierced anyway. She was mad when she saw it and said that she'd told me not to. I said, 'You have no right to tell me not to; it's my tongue. I didn't tell you that you couldn't go buy those shorts you've got on. I don't like them, but it's your butt, so you can do whatever you want with it.' So for the rest of the time that I was living there, both she and my father wouldn't talk to me if they could see the tongue ring in my mouth. He completely took her side." Whether we are dealing with parents, stepparents, or anyone else, it is frustrating when people don't mean what they say. We learn not to trust such people, and trust is essential in a family. When parents feel that it is necessary to change the rules, they need to remember to tell us why. We do not feel compelled to follow rules for which we see no purpose.

The past few stories have brought up another point that deserves emphasis. When our biological parent goes along with our stepparent's arbitrary wishes, we feel betrayed. Biological parents must remember that their children view them as taking sides, unless they explain otherwise. When agreeing with a stepparent's new rules, explain your position to your children. We watch our biological parents hand authority over to our stepparents and it feels unjust, unreasonable, and unfair.

There are several alternatives to disputes over authority. One is for stepparents to assume very little control. Then our relationships with them grow out of something less controversial, like a friendship instead of a contrived parent–child arrangement. This worked very well for Hazel, who had nothing negative to say about her stepmother. "She never tried to impose any rules. She let my dad be the parent and was there to support me without trying to bring her own values into the picture. I think she realized that she couldn't parent me, because I'd pretty much already been raised. There wasn't really anything that she could add to the equation in that sense, so she just tried to be supportive. She was more like my friend; she was very 'sisterly.' She also is eleven years younger than my father, so she's not even old enough to be a parent to me. I think it was pretty smart of her not to try. When I think about when I got in trouble, I can't even see her in the picture; she was just not around. I think if she had tried to discipline me, I probably would have been really evil to her."

Another way to prevent discontent is for our stepparents to make *pleasing* changes in the rules. We welcome our stepparents' ideas about rules and regulations if they work out in our favor. Kara remembered that her stepfather helped her mother be a little more lenient, and that it smoothed her relationship with him: "My mother is incredibly traditional. My stepdad, on the other hand, evens her out beautifully. She sent me to my first day of eighth grade in a three-piece suit. Now, granted, it's sad that my mother was picking out my clothes in eighth grade, but I lived a very sheltered life. She was very old-fashioned and wasn't really caught up with the times. I wanted to wear jeans to school, and she told me I couldn't. I was about fourteen, and this was horrifying to me. My stepfather just looked at her and said, 'What are you doing? She's a big girl!'" Stepparents can be our allies, too.

The struggles we have with our stepparents are usually about much more than just discipline. As several of our interviewees said, their stepparents were reasonable; *they* were the difficult ones, particularly during adolescence! The moral of these stories is that when it comes to disciplining stepchildren, less is usually more. Allowing our parents to call the shots and backing them up is a much more comfortable arrangement for most kids. We appreciate noninvasive support from stepparents; we don't appreciate passive deference from parents who "take her side." The older we are, the more we need our stepparents to be our friends instead of disciplinarians. That allows us to establish relationships built on respect and trust. And, most important, parents and stepparents should remember that growing up is not easy, and we are bound to be cantankerous sometimes. We'll grow out of it.

The answer to the quiz question is A. If you don't want tantrums and rebellion, don't make new rules too early. Children need time to build up trust with someone before they will listen to them as an authority figure. Older stepchildren just need someone who will be their friend. Finding an appropriate role in a new family is very difficult, but if you listen to the family's needs, the change will go more smoothly.

Do I Call Him Daddy?

▼ ▼ ▼ ▼ ▼ ▼ ▼ ▼ ▼ ▼ ▼ ▼ ▼ ▼ ▼ ▼ ▼ ▼

Quiz Question

True or False? If your stepchild calls you by your first name, they love you less than if they called you Mom.

▼ ▼ ▼ ▼ ▼ ▼ ▼ ▼ ▼ ▼ ▼ ▼ ▼ ▼ ▼ ▼ ▼ ▼

(Answer to quiz at end of section)

One might expect that what we call our stepparents would be a good indicator of how we feel about them. One would be wrong. We, Erica and Vanessa, as well as most people we interviewed, call our stepparents by their first names, regardless of how close our relationships are.

The reason is simple: that is how we were introduced, and that is how we referred to them before our parents married them. But there are notable exceptions. Kids who grow up being parented from a young age by their stepparents often call them Mom or Dad instead of by their first names. This pattern holds true in many cases, but it isn't an infallible rule. But then, blended families don't tend to follow any infallible rules!

The name dilemmas don't stop with stepparents. When younger siblings hear their older brothers and sisters use a biological parent's first name, they may adopt the habit. We interviewed one person who called her stepfather, whom she knew as a child, 'Dad,' and her father, whom she met at eighteen, by his name. This brings up a thorny issue: The biological parent may become offended if his or her children begin calling a stepparent by the sacred name Mom or Dad. In our experience, kids avoid such a plight by using those handles only for their biological parents or for someone who has effectively adopted the role of primary caregiver. Relationships in blended families are messy; they are changeable, and they are often undefined, but kids always seem to figure out some taxonomy that works for them. There is no reason for parents to worry about forcing their kids to call the adults by particular names; as long as everyone has a unique identification, things will work out. Here we present some unusual stories, demonstrating that you're not alone, whether the names in your family are "normal" or not.

Simon's family is a prime example of how we adapt to being part of a blended household. He describes how his older half sister influenced him: "I call both my parents by their first names. I picked that up from my older half sister, because I was always around her and she called my dad by his first name. A lot of people are really surprised by it, but my parents have gotten used to it. I don't treat them formally; it's just one of those things." Simon does not sacrifice any closeness with his parents by calling them by their first names, even though it seems strange to outsiders. It is what his family has become comfortable with. When we find a niche that works, we like to stay in it.

Like Simon, Ashley wanted to call her parents the same thing that her siblings did. However, that was a little complicated because she has older half siblings from both her mother's and her father's previous marriages! She told us that all of the children called her father Dad because he really is the male parent to all of them, but that only she and her mother's son call her mother Mom. The situation is confusing to an outsider, but its complexity is normal to her. She said, "My two older brothers do not identify my mom as being their mom, because they were teenagers when she became their stepmother. For two years I called my mom Kim, because that is what my two older brothers did."

For some of us, finding an arrangement that makes us happy is a challenge. Nina had a stepfather by common law, which means that her mother had lived with him long enough that they were considered married by state law. She learned to call him Dad even though she was resistant to the idea. She did not know her father, but she wanted to reserve that title for when she did meet him. But her stepfather was the man who was actually a part of her life, and she told us, "He was the only father that I knew for a really long time. So I called him Dad, but I remember it took me a while to do that. For about a year and a half I called him by his first name. My mom used to get really upset because it would hurt his feelings that I would do that. Eventually I just started calling him Dad to make them happy, and it became habit. It wasn't really something I wanted to do, though. I was very aware of the fact that he was not my father and I didn't feel any need to call him Dad." Even when our parents decide for us which names we'll use, they can't change how we feel about our stepparents.

When remarried parents divorce, stepchildren often lose contact with their former stepparent. What may have been a close parental relationship at one time becomes sadly undefined when the link provided by the biological parent is broken. At that point, what we call our former stepparent becomes more or less irrelevant if there is not a strong relationship between us. Hazel's parents were married, and she has an older half sister from a previous marriage of her mother's. That means that her father is her sister's stepfather. Now that Hazel's parents are divorced, her father and half sister's relationship has changed. She said of her father and her half sister, "Unfortunately, I don't think he ever really thought of my older sister as his daughter. When my mom and dad got divorced, they didn't have anything to keep them in contact. Actually, they see each other occasionally, on big holidays. She calls him Dad, but she has children of her own, and he doesn't think of them as his grandkids."

Even when we do choose to call a stepparent Mom or Dad, it doesn't necessarily make the situation any less complex. Stewart called his stepfather Dad, since his own dad died when he was very young. But he felt a little awkward about it when his stepbrothers would visit, because it was really their father that he was calling Dad. He described how he felt: "The only father that I knew for father-son games and things like that was my stepdad. It was weird because when his real sons came over I realized, 'Oh, now we have to share.' I was young, and no one really explained it to me that well. I thought it was right that I called him Dad because he was the one who *was* dad to me."

In a blended family, relationships that look like they should be easy to understand usually aren't. Greg was ten when his mother remarried, and he called her new husband Dad from the beginning because the man really was his father! However, his feelings toward his father were very similar to those kids often have toward stepparents, because they were getting to know each other when Greg was an older child. He told us, "At first I was really happy. I think it's a dream for a lot of kids. Your parents get divorced, and you always hope that they are going to get back together again. I felt that that was the natural state of things. I was hoping they would get back together, but when they did it was still surprising." Moving in with a man he had only visited occasionally took adjustment for Greg, even though it was his biological father. "We moved to Ireland, and we lived there for a year. It was a hard time because I had not really known my dad. The first year or so it was actually like living with an uncle; I had to get to know him."

The quality of the relationship with a parent or a stepparent is what matters to us, whether or not it is tied to what we call them. Seth told us, "In elementary school my grandfather was really my dad. He had a very stable role in my life as the nurturing male figure. I called him Dad. He died of cancer when I was seven years old, and for me, my dad died that day. I had no idea that I had a natural biological father; I had never seen pictures of him or known that he existed. My grandmother and my mother decided it was time to let me meet my dad, and they told me one day that I was going to meet him. Like I had two dads! The first question out of my mouth was 'What's his name?' I was not going to call him Dad. I knew who Dad was." That summer, Seth met his biological father and stepmother. "I went on the Greyhound bus to see them. I arrived, and they didn't run up and hug me when they saw me. My stepmother actually introduced me to my dad. She told me their names and that they were going to take care of me for the summer. I knew them by their first names. Two weeks into it, I thought my dad, Sam, was the coolest guy in the world! He took me bowling, he taught me how to fish, we went and fed ducks, he taught me how to fly a kite. I was eight years old, and he pulled out this little travel magnet chessboard and taught me how to play chess. At the time it didn't occur to me to wonder what the heck this man was doing in my life. He was a great cook, and one night after dinner I said, 'Sam, thank you for dinner.' I was on my way to my room when Anna turned to me saying, 'You know, you can call him Dad.' I broke down. I ran to my room; I was so confused. I couldn't call him Dad. She came into the room to comfort me, and my dad was just washing dishes. He knew what was going on. Anna felt my confusion. I was scared. I cried a lot. She didn't really know what to say. She couldn't handle me not knowing that he was really my dad. Later he came into the room, and I had my first sex education that night. I found out that he made me, basically, which cleared a few things up. Up until then I had just thought that my dad, who was actually my grandfather, was just older than everybody else's, and I hadn't known why!"

There are many creative ways to avoid too much confusion and hurt feelings. When there aren't enough names to go around, it can help to invent new ones! Suzanne and her siblings worked out their own system. She has a number of both step- and biological siblings, and they all decided to call her stepfather the same thing, which was a name they thought up just for him. She told us, "Everyone calls him Pap. It's great because it's not Dad and it's not Father and it's not a typical name for a father figure. It's just Pap. We have the same respect for him as we would for a father, but for me it's always been true that my dad is going to be my dad whether I like it or not. I can't go back and change that. So we created a word for my stepfather that wasn't Dad. He likes it. It has caught on. Everyone calls him that."

Every blended family will establish its own nomenclature, and no matter what names we pick, what we call our parents and stepparents is always less important than how we feel about them. We understand that for parents, being called "mom" or "dad" holds special significance. For us, the titles often don't matter, and sometimes give no indication of how we really feel. This is another situation where talking explicitly about what makes both parents and children comfortable makes a painful misunderstanding less likely to occur. Parents who worry about what their children call them could be better spending their time talking to their children about how they feel. We suggest inventing your own names, and worrying less about who gets the coveted "dad" or "mom."

The answer to the quiz question is False. How we feel about our parents and stepparents is not always indicated by what we call them.

Not Blood Brothers

▼ ▼ ▼ ▼ ▼ ▼ ▼ ▼ ▼ ▼ ▼ ▼ ▼ ▼ ▼ ▼ ▼

Quiz Question

You and your new spouse both have children. The best way to foster a relationship between the new siblings is to:

a. Force them into many joint activities that you plan for them
b. Make them share bunk beds
c. Threaten them with more chores and less allowance if they can't get along
d. Make sure they each have some private space, and allow them to find what they have in common on their own

▼ ▼ ▼ ▼ ▼ ▼ ▼ ▼ ▼ ▼ ▼ ▼ ▼ ▼ ▼ ▼ ▼ ▼

(Answer to quiz at end of section)

Everybody knows about stepsisters. They are the whiny, cruel, ugly girls who make Cinderella slave away while they preen in vain to steal her prince. They are the ones who won't share their dresses or beads and who have such big, knobby feet that they have to cut off their toes to fit the slipper. Who knows why they seem to like each other's miserable company and yet hate sweet, kind Cinderella? Presumably it's because she's not their real sister, so they figure they can exploit her. Luckily, real stepsisters and stepbrothers are not generally under that delusion.

One of the more unique aspects of a blended family is that we inherit siblings with whom we have no actual blood in common. We are related by the marriage of our parents. With half siblings we have a parent in common, and usually we develop relationships with them that are indistinguishable from those between full, genetic siblings because we know them from birth. Stepsiblings, on the other hand, are children with whom we have no parents in common. They are "married into" our families, and we are "married into" theirs. Often, we are both older when we meet, and we do not share much of our childhoods together. Stepsiblings are a reality of many blended families, and in this section we explore the nature of the relationship between siblings who have completely different parents. As one would expect, many flavors are found in these relationships, ranging from near strangers to best friends.

When we first meet our stepsiblings, we often feel like strangers in a strange land. We do not share a family background or childhood memories, and although we are now linked by our parents' marriage, trying to connect with them immediately can be difficult. Martin ran into some obstacles while trying to get to know his stepsiblings because not only were they new people to him, they didn't speak the same language! He described meeting his stepsiblings: "The first time I met them was on a road trip that we took with my dad and stepmother. It was awkward at first. We had just met, and we were stuck in a car together for the entire summer. They were both teenagers, and their English was good, but not incredibly great. I thought they were nice, and we got along pretty well. But it was difficult to communicate because of the language difference." Luckily, most of us don't have to struggle with a language barrier, but there are plenty of other hurdles to overcome.

One troublesome part of our relationships with stepsiblings is that we may not see them very much. We both have other parents to visit, and often there is an age difference between us which creates more distance. Alex has two older stepbrothers, and he expressed a desire to get closer to them: "I don't know them very well. They were so much older when we all lived at home that I don't have many memories." However, he added jokingly, "I have a vague recollection of them pulling me down and farting in my face when I was four or five. But more recently, I didn't see my brother Mike for about three years because he lived on the East Coast, and he didn't really have money to come visit. I'd see my brother Tom maybe once a year. I really want to get to know them because I think they're smart guys, and I really like both of them. I've been working on spending time with them whenever I can and building a friendship-type relationship with them." But getting to know people you don't see often is never easy. Alex told us, "The last time I saw them was a near disaster. My brother Tom lives in Seattle, and he is married. And my brother Mike lives in Texas. Last November we all flew to Seattle for my uncle's birthday. We got to Tom's apartment, and when I saw Mike, the first thing I said to him was, 'Hey, Mike, you're looking out of shape!' He was really, really, really mad at me. I couldn't believe it came out of my mouth—I don't say mean things like that! I cried for about three hours because I hadn't seen my brother for three years, and I just messed it up. I was so upset. I know it comes from feeling really uncomfortable being around my family, especially after three years apart. We talked about it that weekend. The only time I got to spend alone with them was one dinner before I left, but it is still my goal now to have a better relationship with them."

Large age differences are common culprits in distant sibling relationships, but there is another one: adolescence. Denise is now ten years older and more mature, but she told us, "I was thirteen when my mom married their dad, so I was pretty self-absorbed. They were so far removed from my age that we didn't have much in common. The boy had some hostility toward me because I was living with his dad and he wasn't. And I think that he associated my mom with his parents' divorce. It was irritating for me to be around them, because when they were little, they would act out, and my parents would have to discipline them. Dinner would be a constant battle: 'Eat your food, eat your food.' Then I got older, and every time they would come over to our house I was in an argument with my mom or was leaving. I was a nut case for the first five years that they knew me, and then I went to college. Even now I don't see them much. I have opportunities for siblings that I haven't taken. When I go visit now we can sit down and have conversations; it's fun. They are good kids. I wasn't jealous of them, because my mom wasn't really parenting them, and as far as I was concerned, if my mom paid attention to somebody else, that was fine."

More often than not, we may choose not to become close because we are old enough to know that we aren't compatible. Jay and his stepbrother have no huge friction between them, but they just never really connected. Jay said, "We're friendly, but we don't really talk about anything significant. I don't think that if we did spend a lot of time around each other we'd become great friends. It's not any specific thing about him that I dislike, it's just that we're different people. I don't keep very close tabs on him."

On the other hand, Mark had a personality conflict from the very beginning with his stepmother's children. The problem wasn't that they didn't get to know one another. He told us, "My dad married my stepmother when I was about four, so I lived with my step-brothers for most of my childhood. We were incompatible on every level. They were always in sports and they tried to get me to join, and I was just not interested. I have always been more into school. One of them was an accounting major and went into hotel management. The other one tried to be a pro wrestler or something like that. He took steroids and he would eat only protein and baked potatoes. Plus, I was always interested in boys and they were interested in girls, and so we were complete opposites from the very start of things to the very end."

However, even with stepsiblings who are our opposites, we are not doomed to conflict. Stewart said of his stepbrother, "I respect the younger of my stepbrothers a lot; he's older than me. My real brother and I were brought up to think college was a necessity—that's just what the people who we grew up around did. Neither of my stepbrothers went to college; they have tried different professions, and they've failed a lot, and they've come back up and tried again. My younger stepbrother has always been the nicest guy to me. He is striving to do what he has wanted to do, and he's having a good time. We respect each other; he respects me for being responsible and going to college and jumping through the hoops and taking that route in life. I totally respect him for following his dreams."

Living together, even part-time, significantly helps our relationships become more familiar in tone. For some people, a stepsibling can become as close as a real one. Suzanne recalls that when she first met her stepsister they immediately started play-fighting. "My stepsister is a little bit younger then I am. I was throwing M&Ms at her while she was on the phone with her mom. It wasn't mean, I was just trying to get her attention. She kept saying, 'Knock it off!' into the phone, and her mom was saying, 'I'm not doing anything.' Of course she was saying it to me, not her mom. I was laughing at her, but not in a mean stepsister way. We were just playing." Suzanne found that when her mother and her stepsister's father had married, her mother had less time to spend with her, and she was glad she could turn to her stepsister for a listening ear. "I needed someone else to talk to, so I started talking to my stepsister. She's a very quiet person. *Shy* is not even a good word to describe her; she is beyond shy. I talked to her, and she wouldn't respond. So I talked more. She would nod her head and agree with me, or she'd say, 'Yeah, that sounds sort of cool.' She would just be very quiet and soft. And I'd talk more, telling her whatever was going on in my life. She'd just sit and listen. I thought it was cool, but eventually my goal with her was to get her to talk. She had to start being a person, having feelings. It was driving me up the wall. I understand that some people are built shy, but I am very outgoing and forward, and I could not stand the fact that someone else wasn't like that. I was trying to get her to voice what she wanted and what she liked. Now she can do it, and I'm excited. It's nice to have someone to talk to."

Zoe spent only one year living with her stepsister, who is the same age she is. Even though ninth grade was a difficult year for each of them, she has some fond memories of being very close. "She and I went to England for two weeks to meet my stepfamily there. Most of the time it was just the two of us, and that was really nice. We stayed with her grandmother, who is a ninety-year-old, mostly blind woman who drives a golf cart around this small town outside of London and lives in an old converted pub. She's great. Then we stayed with her aunt. She's kind of proper. Laurie grew up going to her house and being told (in her English accent) 'Not to track anything into the house!' It was an amazing house, with a beautiful garden. It was a fun trip, but it is a strange situation to be suddenly and instantly related to someone with whom you previously had nothing in common."

The fact that we do not share the same family history doesn't get erased, even if we become close to our stepsiblings. We can become as familiar with them as we are with our other siblings, but we cannot rewrite their past. Serena and her stepbrother get along really well, but she knows that she treats him differently than she would a biological brother. "Peter is my middle stepbrother; he's fantastic. He is really funny, charming, and artistic, and he lives in New York on his own. He has quite a romanticized life. I had all my friends over and he got along well with them—a little too well with some of the girls. He would say to them, 'I have so, so much I could show you,' in this sultry tone of voice. I thought, 'Oh, no.' I felt responsible for his behavior, but I feel like I don't get to tell him how to act with women because we haven't grown up together. If it was my own brother, it would be different."

The difference between siblings and friends is that we choose our friends; we don't choose our siblings. We don't choose our stepsiblings either, but because often we don't grow up with them, we treat them more like friends. (That is, when we are getting along!) Jordan describes his time with his stepbrothers as "a big riotous play time" and then adds, "Ethan, the oldest one, and I are still really good friends. We were best friends all throughout high school. We had the same common group of friends. We're friends to this day." Abigail had a similar experience with her stepbrother. She remembers that she and her sister got along very well with her stepbrother when they were young and that they scheduled their visits to Abigail's dad's house so that they could be together. "We liked him. He's a little younger than my sister, but not very much. We were all friends and played together, so we wanted to be at the same house at the same time. We were very close; it was quite idyllic."

Stewart remembers that his stepbrothers seemed like part of a completely different family than his but that they could have a good time together: "My two stepbrothers lived with their mom and her boyfriend, and my brother and I lived with my stepfather and my mom; we were really two separate families. We'd always invite them over for Thanksgiving and Christmas. Very sporadically, they would come by, usually if they needed to pick up something, like a tool, or if they needed money. It was always weird when we hung out, but we are about the same age, so we all liked similar things; we'd always talk and chat. Since we have gotten older we get along better."

One facet of a sibling relationship that often survives the strangeness of being a "step" is good old sibling rivalry. Serena, who is generally very close to her stepsiblings, remembers that it was sometimes hard to get along with her stepsister. She told us how she turned that into a contest: "My mom, my stepdad, my stepbrother Peter, my stepbrother Stephen, Tim, my stepnephew, my stepsister and my brother, all of us, went to New York for a week. We took two cars; Peter was living there, and we met up when we arrived. We did a lot in smaller groups; my brother and I would go off together, or my two stepbrothers would go out together. My stepsister, however, was miserable and let everybody know it all the time. She tried to control the whole group. My stepfather would never say it, but I know he saw how accommodating my brother and I were being, and he realized that his own daughter was being very bratty. She was ruining the trip.

My brother and I recognized that we could play it just a tad. She would whine, 'I don't want to go there; I won't eat that,' and we would say, 'We're happy with whatever you want to do.' We played the 'perfect children' role; we thought it was very funny."

It may sound obvious, but there really is no secret to successful stepsibling relationships. They take time, effort, and a little something in common, just like all other relationships. Noticeably, none of our interviewees reported disliking their stepsiblings just because they are steps; neither was their affection based solely on the fact of their parents' marital status. It's the personality that matters. When our stepsiblings are people we can care about, our relationships with them become rich and rewarding.

The answer to the quiz question is D. Stepsiblings will become close if they have something in common, just like any other children. Parents cannot force a relationship to blossom between stepsiblings.

My Parents Are Married, But My Older Sister's Aren't

▼ ▼ ▼ ▼ ▼ ▼ ▼ ▼ ▼ ▼ ▼ ▼ ▼ ▼ ▼ ▼ ▼ ▼

Review Question

Half siblings have:
  a. Zero parents in common
  b. One parent in common
  c. Two parents in common

d. Three parents in common

▼ ▼ ▼ ▼ ▼ ▼ ▼ ▼ ▼ ▼ ▼ ▼ ▼ ▼ ▼ ▼ ▼ ▼

(Answer to review question at end of section)

Strangely enough, some blended family members have never experienced divorce. They are the children born after remarriage, the younger half siblings who have a stepfamily from birth. Their own parents are married, although of course their older half siblings' parents are not. What is it like to have been born after all the major transitions are over? When these children finally become aware that their brothers and sisters do not have the same set of parents as they do, how do they feel?

Like all children, these children have widely different experiences growing up. Some live with half siblings who are close in age and call their stepparent Mom or Dad, making it tough to notice that theirs is a blended rather than biological family. Others have half siblings who are much older or who leave occasionally to visit their other parent. It's no fun getting left behind when that happens, especially when you don't understand why. Erica remembers when her younger half sister, Kelsey, was beginning to realize that her two big sisters had a different dad. "Vanessa and I were about to leave for our dad's for the weekend as usual. Kelsey asked where we were going, and my mom answered that we were going to Roy's house. Kelsey was just a toddler, but she knew she wanted to do anything Vanessa and I got to do. She began crying, 'I want to go to Roy's! *I* want to go to Roy's house, too.' It has always been hard for her to see us leave all the time."

Kelsey came to understand our family structure when she was very young because she had a lot of clues. For Brian, a twenty-one-year-old science student, the situation was harder to piece together because his half brother's father wasn't around. "Allen just called my dad Dad, and all the fatherly things that needed to be done were done by my dad for both of us. If anyone came up to Allen when he was little and said, 'Go get your dad,' he'd go get my dad. I first figured it out when I realized that Allen had more grandparents than I did. I thought that was pretty unfair. On Christmas we'd go to his grandparents' house, and we'd both eat candy canes over there. But it confused me that somehow they were these beautiful, nice people that were only Allen's and not mine. Allen had grandparents on our mom's side, my dad's side, and Allen's dad's side. He had three sets of grandparents, and I had only two. It was kind of like an extra growth off the family tree, and I didn't really understand it. But it was life, and it explained why he always got more money in his stocking than I did."

Most of us regard our siblings as just plain old brothers and sisters, regardless of their formal status. Referring to them as real sisters and brothers comes naturally, and we know that rescinding the title is hurtful. Brian went on to report, "Once when I was little, I got really mad at Allen, and I yelled, 'You're not my real brother,' because I had just figured that out. But I never did that again." The fact that Allen has a different father has made little difference in their relationship, both then and now. "Because he's so much older, when my friends came over we would always play us versus Allen, but that was just to equalize things. Our relationship has been more affected by our age difference than by not being in the same genetic family. If it's going to be obvious to someone that he's not really my brother, then I'll explain more. But if they're not going to know, then I'll just leave it at that. Because it's not really a bad description. In all ways but name he really is my brother."

Simon agreed. He said of his older half sister, "I always just called her my sister. That's all. We've always been that close. I never made the distinction that she was my half sister." Simon's (half) sister was also quite a bit older, which meant he had someone other than his mom and dad to spoil him and show him the ropes. "When she went to college I got to spend a lot of time with her. She'd pamper me. She'd show me college life; it was really fun. My parents eat very healthy, but when I visited her, she would always give me all these treats." As older sisters who are also safely away at college, Vanessa and Erica know how fun it is to suggest mischief to our comrade on the home front. Vanessa once tried to get ten-year-old Kelsey to recite her sex education worksheets at dinner, but Kelsey just laughed.

Even when younger half siblings are aware that their parent's first family exists, they may find it difficult to really imagine. Simon remembered the day that he talked to his mother and finally understood her "other life" before he was born. "I saw her in a different light. I'd never really heard her talk about her other husband before. Every once in a while she'd make something funny out of it, but besides that I never knew much about the relationship. It gave me a different perception of this person, not just as my mother, but as someone who can make the same mistakes I can." That is something we all learn, one way or another. Children of blended families may learn of their parent's fallibility sooner than other children because we live with the reality of a divorce: the painful result of an admitted mistake. Surprisingly, we feel that knowledge of our parent's mistakes has actually helped us mature, by making us realize at a young age that no one is perfect. For children whose parents have been married since they were born, understanding the significance of the past can be more difficult. Children such as Simon, who grew up with older half siblings, are caught somewhere in the middle. Their parents are married, but their half siblings remind them that theirs is a complex family history.

Sophie, who speaks fluent Chinese and likes to travel, remembers a sense of unreality about her older half sister's other family. "Her dad is married again and has two sons. I remember being jealous of her when she was in college that she had brothers, because I always wanted brothers. I never met her family because she would go away to see them; they never came here to see her. But then both her families would go to her college to see her, and I finally met her brothers; they finally existed for me. They're really cute; they have red hair. They don't look anything like her, and I look a lot like her. I guess even now that part of her family doesn't seem exactly real to me. I can't relate her to it very well."

Sophie was the one who caused mischief in her family, and she managed to drag her half sister, Amanda, into it. "I got a D on my English packet, and if you got lower than a C you had to get a parent signature. I was scared to forge my mom's signature, so I forged Amanda's signature. Of course the teacher called my mom because the teacher was wondering, 'Who is this Amanda person?' I don't know why I thought that Amanda would be vested with enough authority for me to even bother forging her signature in the first place, but my mom's signature was a sacred thing, and I couldn't forge that. I got in big trouble with my mom for doing it."

Despite the childhood pranks, a parent couldn't ask for two siblings to get along better than Sophie and Amanda do. Sophie continued, "I admired her so much. Everything she did was the coolest. She had a jean jacket with buttons all over it, and then she put some of the buttons on the inside. I don't know why she liked me, but when I was fourteen she decided that she liked me, and so I'd go visit her every New Year's. Now she lives only two hours away from where I go to school, so I go visit her a couple times a year. She's the most laid-back person that I've ever met. She painted her floor bright blue like a street sign—a hardwood floor! She's really artistic, and she has good taste, and her house is very homey and comfortable. She just wears jeans and a T-shirt and somehow manages to look really classy and nice all of the time. She's just neat." Amanda and her husband now have a baby daughter, and they are deciding what the child will call Sophie's father. "Amanda calls my dad George. My dad had this plan for a while that the baby was going to call him Grumps. Instead of Gramps, Grumps. My dad's weird, but anyway, I think the baby's going to call him Grandpa George."

Sophie related a family anecdote about her father trying to win over her older half sister. "Apparently my dad really wanted to get in good with Amanda when he first married my mom. He would wake them both up with a cup of coffee and a back rub. He did this every morning. Now she's the biggest coffee addict you've ever met! She drinks more coffee than anyone I know, and I think it's all my dad's fault. They get along really well." Amanda corroborated the story: "It's true. He was an early riser, and my mom and I were always sleeping late and being really groggy."

Younger half siblings often have to learn about family events after the fact. Ashley, an animated nineteen-year-old and younger half sister to three boys, knows that she represented a large shift in the family when she was born. She said of her older brothers, "I think for a long time they felt torn, because they loved me to death, but they had trouble adjusting to my parents getting married, and on top of that there was a new baby. It was a bonding time for them, and I didn't have that experience. I can remember being eight or nine and my brothers calling me a spoiled brat, and I was; I really was. We'd never had money prior to that time because my dad had been going to medical school and slowly working his way up. Then finally my dad started to make some more money. All of a sudden I was getting new clothes and being allowed to do things I hadn't been able to do before. I didn't ask for it; I was so young that I didn't realize what was happening. My brothers were old enough to realize, though, and it bothered them that I took it for granted."

Regardless of what many parents may think, sibling rivalry is no fun for kids, and a lot of us are glad to avoid it. Blended families often provide a special opportunity for us to have siblings with whom we get along because we don't live with them every day. Christina is a twenty-year-old interested in studying child development. She said of her half brother, "Because he wasn't in my life all the time, it was always really awesome when he was there. We never fight, and we get along really well. He always played with me when he was visiting, so I only had the really positive aspects of my brother and never the negative aspects." Christina's half sister explained the family situation to her when she was quite young. "I think when I was around four or five, I realized that my sister wasn't my full sister. I knew it was somehow similar to Cinderella and the stepsisters. I couldn't figure out what she was, so I asked her if she was my stepsister, and she said no. Then it was explained to me that she was my half sister, and that was what I called her." Christina's older half sister often vacationed with her own father, and when we asked how that affected Christina she replied, "She is so much older than me that it didn't ever cross my mind to be jealous. It made sense that she was doing it because she was older, and I was too little to be going to those places and doing those things."

Christina remembers that her two older half siblings were very innovative in coming up with ways to keep her occupied. "There was one game we used to play, which they invented so that they could have time together and not really have to play with me. But I would think that they were playing with me. I really liked the game; it was fun and creative. Our bunk beds would be a ship, and we would be sailing to some destination. I was supposed to steer the ship, and so I was on the bottom bunk, and they hung out on the top bunk and did whatever they wanted. They were going to tell me when they spotted land. I just waited and played by myself, and they hung out on the top deck. When they decided it had been long enough, we would go outside and explore the new territory. So I would go and explore new territory, and they would go and explore some other new territory together. But it was fun. We didn't fight, and they never actually said, 'No, you can't play.'"

Christina remembers when she began wondering about the fact that her brother didn't live with her. "Since I was raised in that world, that was just what I accepted as normal. I think at some point I questioned why he only visited and didn't stay, but it took me a long time, experiencing other things and reading books, to start thinking, 'Oh, maybe my brother's visiting isn't quite what everybody does.' Christina's words express a common experience. Most of us see our own families as normal, no matter what quirky configuration they have, because that is what we have grown up knowing.

We pay little attention to genetic ties when deciding who to love as a brother or sister. The younger half siblings whom we spoke to had a difficult time remembering to refer to their older siblings as "half." It is usually true that half siblings don't spend as much time together as regular siblings, so we often appreciate each other more when we do get to see each other. Having more siblings is one of the happiest consequences of a blended family.

The answer to the review question is B. Half siblings have one parent in common. Stepsiblings have zero parents in common, and as far as we know, it is impossible to have three parents in common.

Twice as Many Holidays, Twice as Many Presents

▼ ▼ ▼ ▼ ▼ ▼ ▼ ▼ ▼ ▼ ▼ ▼ ▼ ▼ ▼ ▼ ▼

Quiz Question

Your holidays will be merriest if you:
  a. Fight incessantly with your ex spouse about who gets the kids
  b. Let your children stay with their other family for the whole holiday, and then call them and complain about how lonely you are
  c. Find out what your ex-spouse is giving your children, and then buy them something more impressive

d. Consult with both your children and their other family when making plans, and try to work out a schedule that everyone can agree on

▼ ▼ ▼ ▼ ▼ ▼ ▼ ▼ ▼ ▼ ▼ ▼ ▼ ▼ ▼ ▼ ▼

(Answer to quiz at end of section)

Although we have not concentrated on the process of divorce per se, there is no denying that divorce is a big factor in blended families. Divorce has many long-term repercussions, among them the subjects of the next two discussions: holiday traditions and financial and legal arrangements. Sometimes our stepparents are directly involved in these matters, and sometimes they are not; nevertheless, both are conspicuous parts of our experiences as children of blended families. Rather than give a prescription for "How to Have a Successful Blended Family Holiday," we will discuss how our families negotiate their time with us and how we feel about the arrangements. The way we handle our holidays says a lot about how well our parents are able to communicate with each other and with us. Most of us find that when the holidays roll around we have a long list of family members who would love to spend time with us, a fact that doesn't often get discussed in the books about divorce.

Vanessa and Erica think of multiple Christmases as one of the best aspects of their blended family childhoods—certainly the most memorable! We've been known to push the total celebrations per year up to four or five: one with our dad; one with our mom, stepdad, and half sister; one with our grandma and extended family; one with our stepgrandparents; and one with family friends. Try to top that! So many celebrations (and so many gifts!) made us feel like everyone's favorite kids. Erica comments, "There was a rule in our family: We always spent Christmas morning at my mom's and went to my dad's at about one in the afternoon. Our parents were very respectful of that arrangement and never questioned that we would see both of them each holiday. I remember feeling sad for my dad, because he didn't get to see us do the 'wake up on Christmas morning' routine. But then I realized that the routine itself wasn't that important, and that my dad, my sister, and I had established our own traditions. Vanessa and I always liked dragging our holidays on for days."

Many of us must travel on the holidays so that everyone gets to see everyone else. However, some families take a different route. Ben had particularly inclusive holiday traditions that incorporated his entire blended family. He described them for us: "We all have Thanksgiving together. Christmas Eve I would have with my mom, and then in the morning we would all drive down and spend the day with my dad. A couple of years my dad came up to my mom's place, and we celebrated Christmas together. My stepfather was there, and some other people too, close friends who are like family. It seemed like everybody else's parents hated each other after they got divorced, or at least didn't see each other. But it was always fine for us; it was never weird. I was totally comfortable. Everyone seemed to get along. It worked."

In addition to requiring divorced parents who can still enjoy each other's company, arrangements such as Ben's clearly demand planning. For some families, that is the stumbling block to cooperation. Allison remembers holidays being very disorganized. "Everything was really haphazard. It always seemed that whatever system we had was set up so that everybody would come away offended. That's the best I can possibly put it. It was generally respected among everybody that Jewish holidays should be spent with the Jewish side of the family and Christian holidays with the other side. Basically we all tried to make it so that whenever somebody wanted a holiday with the kids, they got it. But it always went wrong somehow. Inevitably, somebody was angry, or we wouldn't make it where we were supposed to go; there was always some dumb catastrophe." Everybody knows that cooperation isn't easy, especially for ex-spouses. But Allison's story shows us how important it is, for the sake of everyone's sanity. If parents are unable to work together, even for our sake, the holidays can be filled with tension. The trouble it takes for parents to cooperate on making plans that work for us is usually less than the animosity that results from a lack of organization.

Like Allison, Mark had two different religious traditions to contend with, but he didn't see that as a problem. It was actually a perk. He said, "Because my mom is Jewish, I had eight days of Hanukkah, and then five days of Christmas at my dad's. I had it all. That was another point of contention among my friends—I was 'the half Jew.' They celebrated Christmas, so they would ask, 'How can you have both?' It was the biggest reason why I had to explain my family to everybody, because I celebrated more than one holiday during that time, and they didn't understand it. Their attitude was, 'One or the other, please.' For me it was fun. I had a lot of holidays growing up: all the Christian ones, all the Jewish ones."

Parents have to do the logistical planning when the children are small, but that changes as we grow up. By the time we are in high school and college, we usually manage our own schedules. That can be both a relief and a burden; as always, with freedom comes responsibility. Rosa plans her own holiday travel itinerary, and while she is happy to decide where she will go, she finds that her family isn't always happy with her decisions. She told us, "It is kind of a problem because everybody wants me to spend all my time with them, so I basically have to say, 'Okay, this is what I am doing. I'm sorry if it's not what you wanted.' I went home for Christmas break, and I basically spent it all with my dad just because I get along with him better; my mother and I don't really get along. But I usually stay with her for a little while."

Holidays are hectic already. Once we are deciding for ourselves where we spend our days, fitting in time to see all our many family members can be a trick. Serena said, "Since my dad's marriage, his wife's family has totally taken us in; I mean, they want us to come to every single family gathering. It's crazy at Christmastime because my brother and I spend Christmas Eve with my stepmother's family, then Christmas morning with my mom and my stepdad, and the afternoon is with my dad and stepmom again. We go all these places because they want us there. It is better than not feeling wanted by anybody."

Blended families are often bigger families, which means two things. We have to work a lot harder to see and spend time with everyone, but we also have a lot of people to love us. Of course, that is true every day in blended families, not just on holidays. As Serena said, the planning and traveling are worth it, because there is nothing more important than feeling wanted. Holidays are a striking example of an everyday fact about our families: We have more than one place to go, and we have to work together to get there. Every blended family has to find the system that works for them, and that may be hard at first. This is another situation that calls for a lot of communication between parents, especially when the children are young. It is easy for parents to make holidays an unhappy chore for us by not respecting each other's time. We know blended family parents also face many challenges, not the least of which is how to spend Christmas morning alone before the children arrive! But dividing up the time fairly and getting along with an ex-spouse long enough to make sure that children are taken care of are essential to having holidays that work for everyone. Once these obstacles have been overcome, which they usually are, holidays can be a time just to enjoy our families.

The answer to this question is D. Holidays run more smoothly when everyone knows what the plan is and has had some say in how it came about. Children need to feel wanted and loved by their families but not nervous about their parents fighting over them.

Bribes, Child Support, and Legal Matters

▼ ▼ ▼ ▼ ▼ ▼ ▼ ▼ ▼ ▼ ▼ ▼ ▼ ▼ ▼ ▼ ▼ ▼

Quiz Question

True or False: Parents should take responsibility for making financial and legal arrangements that work without relying on their children to be go-betweens.

▼ ▼ ▼ ▼ ▼ ▼ ▼ ▼ ▼ ▼ ▼ ▼ ▼ ▼ ▼ ▼ ▼ ▼

(Answer to quiz at end of section)

Most people would probably rather avoid thinking about all the messy financial and legal issues that arise in divorced and remarried families. We know it's no fun, but if not handled well, these issues can cause a lot of heartache. Raising children is hard work, and the paradox is that divorced parents have to make even more effort to work together than married parents do, because they have to negotiate child support and custody arrangements. Not surprisingly, it is much easier on the kids when their parents are able to work cooperatively. The next question is how much children should know about and be involved in money and legal matters. There are several opinions in the stories that follow, but in general kids want to know what the agreement is without being responsible for carrying it out. Children in blended families have enough to worry about without having to make sure the child support is on time or the visitation schedule is followed.

Laura was an only child growing up, and she felt like she was the messenger between her two very polarized households, one with her mom and one with her dad and stepmother. She was the only link between them. "Their lives are so different. I never wanted to cause any stir; I just wanted everything to be very proper and neat so that nobody would have any reason to be upset about anything. The only contact that my parents had with each other was over money. My mom had me tell my dad when the child support was late. Any back-and-forth was through me, which was obviously not an ideal way for it to be." Asking a child to proctor her own living arrangements can make her feel like a burden or an unwanted reminder of a life past. When a child sees her parents cooperating and communicating in spite of their attitudes toward each other, it makes her feel cared for.

Serena readily remembers her parents' divorce settlement and child support setup: "They never believed in bickering. The divorce settlement was one of the easiest divorce settlements ever. My dad asked my mom how much she needed. And she replied that her lawyer was telling her to ask for more than she really needed. So they compromised. They were very nice to each other. My mom said the one thing about divorce that you should always remember is that you love your kids more than you hate each other, no matter what. When I started college, neither of them was remarried yet, and my mom was worried because she didn't have a very big salary as a teacher. It was hard because I went to a very expensive school, and they both had to figure out how to pay for it. They helped each other out. My dad said he would pay three-fourths and she could pay one-fourth of the cost, and they agreed on that. Things have worked out, and my mom feels less stressed about it since she has been remarried."

By contrast, Tanya's father was reluctant to pay child support when she was a child. Then he married her stepmother, who helped bridge the gap between Tanya and her father for a while. But now they are divorcing, which is difficult for Tanya, although she maintains a close relationship with her stepmother. She told us, "When I applied to college my dad was upset about the cost. But then my stepmom told me that he was really excited that I got accepted to such a good school, and really excited that the school gave me enough financial aid to work with his child support. So for a while things were looking up. He would mail me a check every couple of weeks, and he would call me. He even sent me a card. Then suddenly it stopped about five or six months ago, I think because of his divorce. My dad has always had the attitude that my mom was getting the money and that she was using him. When I was little, sometimes when my mom was at work I would call him to ask for my child support; because it's me, the money goes to me." Tanya struggles because she can't count on either financial or emotional support from her father. Unfortunately, many people confuse the two. Tanya could understand if her father couldn't afford to send her money, but that is not the problem. He doesn't want to be in contact with her, and that is hard for any daughter to understand. We don't equate money with love, and it is the latter that we really want, not the former.

Many parents who pay child support worry that the money won't actually go to help their children. It would seem that once we are old enough to leave home, things would be simpler, because our living expenses are more clear-cut, and we can receive the checks ourselves. But that just doesn't seem to be the case. Nora remembers a particularly confusing money situation: "My first year in college my dad would send his child support to me. I was living in the dorms, so I didn't need the money that he would send. I would send it to my mother. Every month I would deposit it and write her a check, and she used it for my school expenses. I couldn't convince him to just send her the check. It was absurd. But then at some point I started living in my first real house, and I needed the money. My mom relinquished control of it." It is clear that blended families, like all families, require trust in order to operate. Nora's father could have sent the child support directly to her school, or worked out another method by which to ensure that the money got to her.

Trusting your ex-spouse with child support money would be ideal, but if common sense tells you it is out of the question, the next best method is to find ways of paying that take the responsibility off of your children.

Nora preferred to be in control of her financial support once she was living on her own, but as children, we don't want that responsibility. Some parents may think that being involved in the family's finances will help us learn about money and the cost of living at a young age, but even that can go wrong, as we learned from Alex. He didn't have much good to say about his family's money arrangements; "The worst is when they start telling you about finances. I was living with my mom in junior high, and my dad was garnering her wages because she didn't pay any child support when I lived with him. She is probably the most irresponsible person I know with money. Unfortunately, I've picked up a lot of habits from her. My dad is on top of things."

Money quickly becomes a big problem when it's not handled well, but thankfully, many parents are able to deal responsibly with the challenge. When they do, we kids may not have to take notice, which is a blessing. Zoe described the financial situation her parents had: "Neither of them saw any point in complicating things any further, and neither of them wanted to deal with lawyers anymore. I don't think they were ever malicious or spiteful towards each other. At least that aspect of our lives they just dealt with maturely." Rebecca is also thankful for her very cooperative parents. She says of her mother, "I think she was kind of unusual at that time in not asking for alimony. They both had degrees, and they both were going to be earning approximately the same amount of money. She figured out a reasonable amount for him to contribute to my living expenses, and they also saved money for my college tuition."

If divorce creates complicated financial situations, what happens when parents remarry? The situation may get more complicated still, but for many families, the return to a two-earner household is worth it. The question is, how much should a stepparent financially support a stepchild? The answer to that question depends on many factors and cannot be decided by anyone other than the family members involved. If the stepparent is supporting his or her stepchild, it is important for the child to know that she is not a burden, that the responsibility was adopted voluntarily and willingly out of love for her and her parent. Similarly, if the stepparent is not financially supporting his or her stepchild, the child should know that it does not mean that her stepparent cares about her any less. Communication and reassurance are important if we are to understand and feel secure in our families.

Many of us grew up being supported by generous stepparents; they were the ones who put a roof over our heads, paid for our doctor's bills, and bought us ice cream cones. As we get older, we become aware of the commitment that such actions exemplify, and we value the emotional as well as the material support. Stewart told us about how his relationship with his stepfather is different because of that everyday presence. "My stepbrothers go to him and just ask for money. They will flat out say, 'I need five hundred dollars.' I don't feel that I can say that. But he pays for the things I have, constantly. He pays the bills, the mortgage on the house we live in, things like that. My stepbrothers have never lived in our house. He provided for me on an everyday basis, and not only financially; he was here physically all the time. They didn't get that side of the bargain. He wasn't there for them. When they got older they could ask for money because it was the compensation for the care and attention I received when I was younger. That is my take on it." We don't envy Stewart's stepbrothers. Money is not a substitute for attention. In this situation, Stewart is clearly the lucky one, receiving both financial and emotional support.

Seth also told a very poignant story about the relationship between love and money in a blended family. Seth did not know his father as a child, and he said, "My dad's new wife helped him want to be a father again, but he knew that if he saw me, my mother would ask for child support. He knew he couldn't pay it then, but he was prepared to pay for it later, when he did have the money. He was willing to risk it, so he did it. He saw me when I was two. But that was the last time for five years. They wouldn't let him see me because he wasn't paying. He felt bad about that, and he quit trying to see me after a while." Seth's father faced the same fear as Tanya's father: contact with the children equals full financial support. Children need to have relationships with all their parents; money should never get in the way. Making those relationships work when there are financial disagreements or debts will take extra effort. Do it anyway. Parents should neither avoid their children nor prevent their children from seeing their other parent because of money. Happily, Seth now has a close relationship with his father.

The other common issue related to money in divorced families is bribery. Parents may be tempted to give large gifts to their children at the time of a divorce in an attempt to make their lives easier. Perhaps *bribery* is too harsh a word for this impulse, because we can all understand a parent who just wants to do something to make a child happy, especially in the midst of confusing, sometimes scary, changes. Margarita said that when parents divorce, "They're going to do something to spoil you. My dad took my brother and me to Hawaii for Thanksgiving when I was sixteen. We knew something was wrong. He was losing it; you could see that he was determined to hang out with the kids. I think he felt a lot of guilt about the way things were going." But once again, remarriage changes the picture. Margarita continued, "But then when parents have someone new, their attentions shift to the other person. I think that person distracts them from the pain of what's going on, from the guilt they feel towards their children. As uncomfortable as it is when your parents feel guilty and freaked out, there is a way that your identity as parent and child is preserved and celebrated after a divorce because they have no one else." It is clear that we appreciate being the focus of our parent's attention. However, parents should be warned that we can tell if they are spoiling us out of guilt or treating us well because they want to make us happy. That doesn't mean that we don't enjoy getting presents, but we know where they are coming from, even when they don't tell us outright. Giving presents during a difficult time is fine, and we especially appreciate it when it is accompanied by a verbal expression of apology, sympathy, or understanding.

Abigail told us a story of peace offerings from her stepfather. "We got along most of the time, but we had a couple of big fights that lasted for days. He would want me to do something I didn't want to do. It was usually something like taking a coat with me when I went to my friend's house. I would refuse because I didn't want a coat, I wasn't going to go outside, and it seemed like a stupid thing for him to make me do. I was being obnoxious and thirteen. He'd get really angry and scream at me for a while and not let me go to the friend's house. Then it would all blow over, and he would buy me something to make up for it, usually a lamp or a clock. Always appliances." This is not to suggest that bribery is the way to a child's heart; attention will do the trick too!

Unfortunately, money fights, ugly in themselves, can escalate into lawsuits. Our attitude on this one is cut-and-dried: leave us out of it. If parental bickering is hard on children, parental bickering through lawyers is even worse. Lucy told us about the lamentable consequences when a parent *is* the lawyer. "My stepdad and my father are both lawyers so they would write mean lawyer letters to each other. Accidentally, I found one to my father on the computer. I think he had wanted family counseling or something, but my stepfather didn't want anything to do with it. There was also some rotten comment about refusing to pay for something. My stepdad was really angry and basically said to my father that he was not to ever communicate with my mother except through her lawyer—him." Granted, Lucy's parents didn't say that in front of her, but whether these bitter words were accidental or not, hearing them hurts.

Hazel remembers that her parents were careful to keep her out of the child support disputes that came up when she moved from her mother's house to her father's. "My mother had legal custody of me, and my father had partial custody, visitation rights on the weekends. He had a specific amount of child support that he had to pay to my mother for my sister and me. Then I wanted to go to high school where my dad lived, so I went to live with him, and they had to work out a new method of paying child support because my father was supporting me. They went to a lawyer to mediate their new child support arrangement. They were very wise to keep me out of that. I think that is the only place where they got into ugly disputes. I think they also made a pact with each other not to talk about the mediation while it was happening, because they figured it would be hard for me to take." Hazel's parents were wise in their decision to keep her out of the case, because they knew her well enough to predict what she would be comfortable with. They were also responsible enough to settle their differences as adults, without putting Hazel into the middle of their conflict.

Lawrence tries to stay out of his parents' lawsuits, but that too is hard. "My father has sued my mother twice. I hear bad things from my mother about what terrible schemes my father is up to. In many ways it would better if I didn't hear it, but I can't empathize and help my mother if she doesn't tell me how she feels about what's going on. They try to keep my brother and sister out of it, although a few times our father has tried to get us to persuade my mother to take less money, but that is rare. It's generally better when we stay out of it." It is never acceptable to drag your children into a legal battle for the purpose of making them take a side. However, as Lawrence points out, it is okay for parents to tell their children how they feel about the conflict. Being caught in the middle is never easy, but our ability to handle such a problem increases as we get older.

As if it's not enough that all these battles are over *us*, they also make everyday life rather troublesome. Meredith remembers that when her dad remarried, the battles over custody of her and her sister got particularly intense. "When I was around twelve the battles really started in earnest. Dad calls it 'The Custody Case,' and Mom calls it 'When Your Father Sued Me.' My dad wanted the setup to be that we lived at his house all week and then three weekends out of the month we were at our mom's. He also wanted more child support from my mom. My mom wanted half-and-half time. Basically what happened is that dad won. He is just that kind of person; 'Dad Lost' is not a paradigm that actually exists. As soon as it was decided, they totally threw the agreement out the window because, you know, you can't really keep to a rigid schedule; people's lives don't work like that. They never followed the rules correctly, and there were a lot of hard feelings and arguing between them. Then my mom moved to another state when I was a teenager, and it got even worse because my dad felt that she had given up all custody rights by moving. He felt that any time that he granted her was King Dad granting a largesse to this horrible, evil peasant woman. My mom felt that she was automatically entitled to all time that wasn't school time because she never got to see us. It was just a huge steaming bowl of stupidity until I left, and it's now just a big huge steaming bowl for my sister, and I really don't have to deal with it anymore. I will say that my life significantly improved once I was no longer in the twin gravity pull of the custody disagreement." Anyone who has experienced living in two families can understand the twin gravity pull.

The upshot of all this is that kids are happier when financial and legal issues don't turn into battles resembling World War III. Well-mannered cooperation and honest communication make the children feel cared for and prized. No one wants to be the cause of bitter disputes between people they love. Diplomatic discussions may come easily for some, but for others they will require a great deal of effort and discipline. In our opinion, children are worth it.

The answer to the quiz question is True. We do not want to be part of legal disputes, ever. We do not want to watch our parents fight over money, and we do not want to be a referee.

The Name Game

▼ ▼ ▼ ▼ ▼ ▼ ▼ ▼ ▼ ▼ ▼ ▼ ▼ ▼ ▼ ▼ ▼ ▼

Quiz Question

You and your children have different last names. Your children will most likely:

- a. Be horribly embarrassed
- b. Get very angry and impatient with anyone who calls them by the wrong name
- c. Correct people who make a mistake but overall be relatively unaffected
- d. Think their family is grossly abnormal

▼ ▼ ▼ ▼ ▼ ▼ ▼ ▼ ▼ ▼ ▼ ▼ ▼ ▼ ▼ ▼ ▼ ▼

(Answer to quiz at end of section)

We are all familiar with the derogatory adjectives used to describe a divorced family. We say they are a "broken home" or a "troubled family"; even having a single mom has negative connotations. Remarriage repairs some of those social stigmatizations, but not without costs. What we gain in perceived social stability is mitigated by the confusion we cause in the minds of those around us:

Whose last name do you have? Who exactly are you related to? What do you mean, you celebrate both Hanukkah and Christmas? Why are there three people at school on Parents' Night? Blended families are complicated webs, and the "real," genetic links are often not where you would expect them to be. That is a testament to the fact that we form our families based on bonds that are emotional, not chemical. For kids who grow up in blended families, the complexity is normal. Explaining it to the uninitiated can be a chore, but one that teaches us patience, sensitivity, and poise.

Names are tools of communication, symbols we use to identify one another. Conventional rules regarding family names are evolving quickly today, in part as a result of blended families. Yet the norms are not forgotten, and we are always conscious when we break them. Here we discuss two issues: how names figured in our lives, and how explaining our family setups to others affected us. They are two sides of the same coin, both giving us a glimpse of how children of blended families perceive themselves and their families. Our names are our identities: both our most private and our most public possessions.

Nina grew up living with her mother and stepfather. She has her mother's last name, which became somewhat of an issue when her father reentered her life after her seventeenth birthday. "My birth certificate has only her name. It doesn't have his at all, which is kind of amazing because he was there when I was born, but she never wrote it down. When I met my dad, my mom actually tried to get me to switch my last name. I think she was trying to give him credit. She told me that it was fine if I wanted to take his last name, it wasn't going to bother her. But it wasn't what I wanted, so I didn't. It was my mom's way of telling me that it was okay for me to be with my father without her actually having to say it." Nina's story shows that names are powerful symbols not only of our origins, but also of the history we build throughout our lives.

Traditionally, the only people who worried about changing their last names were newly married women. In that case, names are symbols of the future as much as of the past. When talking about blended families, name-changing affects children too. A mother getting remarried may no longer have the same last name as her children. That very scenario occurred in our family, and Erica recalls, "I got used to my mom's new name right away; it didn't bother me that we suddenly had different last names. In fact, I would always correct people who called her by her old name." Vanessa was only seven when it happened: "Our mom used to have our last name? I don't remember that."

Different last names may cause some logistical problems, but usually such problems are easily solved. Rebecca remembers, "My mom kept her name, and I have my father's name, and my stepfather has another name. In a way, it was cool. I felt like we were this family with fifty thousand names. Sometimes we had students living with us who rented out a room, and then we would have another name in the family. I never felt weird about it, but issues came up at school when someone would sign my permission slip and the teacher didn't recognize the name. Nowadays lots of families have different names, but back then it was slightly more unusual for a mom to keep her name. People had a little more trouble dealing with it. I would just say, 'You moron, that's my mom!' It was their problem to figure it out."

Understanding the web of names and relationships in a blended family is not hard, if they have been explained well enough. But without an explanation, outsiders may make assumptions are that are often wrong. For that reason, blended family members find themselves perpetually clarifying the family tree—or not! Abigail told us about how they use the multitude of last names in her two families to their advantage: "My sister and I have my dad's last name, Finnegan. But my mom doesn't, and neither does my stepmom; they both have their own last names. So people will call and ask for Mrs. Finnegan—at both houses—and everyone knows that if it is for Mrs. Finnegan, then it's somebody selling something, and we say we're not interested and hang up. It's hard for people who try to find us by looking in the phone book, but it usually works out."

Some people choose to avoid the confusion by keeping an old name. When Serena's mother got remarried, she kept her first married name as her middle name and tacked her new last name onto the end. For Serena and her siblings that was a nice surprise because it meant they could still borrow her credit cards! Serena told us, "She had been a Randall for so long, and she said, 'It's as much my middle name as anything else I've ever known.' I thought it was awesome that she could do that." But sometimes that seemingly simple strategy may add to the chaos. As Mark told us, "I have my dad's last name. My mom's kept it, too. Incidentally, I think three of my dad's wives have kept the last name, and they all live in the same city, so I can imagine people are confused."

Different people react differently to mistaken assumptions about their families. For some children it is an issue of great importance that everyone understand, and others would rather avoid public explanations. Then again, sometimes our attempts to clarify fall on deaf ears. Nora recalls explaining her family to a younger cousin: "She was six and I was seven. We were sitting on her bed, and she said, 'Jack's your father now.' I said 'No. No, he's not. He's my mom's husband, and he's my stepfather. But he's not my father,' and then I explained who my father was. She said, 'No, the one that your mother is married to is your father,' and she had a very condescending tone of voice like she was really clear about all of this and she definitely knew what was going on. I knew she was the younger one and I was supposed to be calm about this stuff. I just said, 'No, Caitlyn. You're wrong about this one. I have a father.' She got really pissed off at me and put her dolls down and looked at me. Then she explained the whole thing to me again. I just walked out of the room. I didn't say anything about it, and, oddly enough, I didn't tell my mom. I didn't get mad. But she is now twenty-one years old, and I still remember it."

Not all children are as stubborn as Nora's cousin; most are just curious. Mark recounts how his friends reacted to his not-so-nuclear family: "All of my friends had married parents and traditional families. So they would say, 'Which house is Mark at today?' I always had to explain myself, and they've always asked questions and been curious because they didn't know what it was like. We lived in a suburb filled with nuclear families, and the fact that I didn't have one made me a little different. My friends thought it was cool because I always got to have two rooms and two piles of things and money from both sides."

Misunderstandings are easily remedied with information. Although patiently explaining our families for the two-hundredth time may be tedious, it is relatively painless. What really hurts is when people look down on us because of our blended families. Seth was raised by his mother and grandparents. He remembers that as a child his family setup was not looked well upon by his community. "They thought it was different. The reason my teachers let it go was that my grandmother was the principal of the school. She had started the school, and she had no problem with it. People didn't think my family was 'healthy.' But I turned out just fine. Back then I thought my family *was* normal." Luckily, most people we interviewed never had to deal with a truly hostile environment.

School plays an important role, because for most children it is where they first encounter the world without their parents. The peers and other adults that we interact with at school may be unfamiliar or uncomfortable with what we have taken for granted all our lives, and their attitude will have an effect on us. Lawrence's parents were married when he started school. "At the boarding school that I went to, they screened people out who came from divorced families. I'd imagine that if you were a super-good student they would probably let you in, but I didn't meet a single student from an untraditional family. I remember when I applied being asked, 'Are your parents still married?' Most of my friends didn't care; it was faculty and administrators who disapproved of it." Lawrence said that when his own parents divorced and subsequently remarried other people, he had to change his perception of blended families. "It bothered me a little bit that others would see me as a kid with a screwed-up family, but that didn't last long. I remember when I was a child, my parents told my siblings and me that we should never marry people who came from troubled families. So we joked about the fact that now no one should marry *us*!"

Jordan's world was quite the opposite of Lawrence's. He said, "I only knew one kid whose parents were actually married. That was weird to me. It's scary—they've been together fifty years! They must drive each other crazy." The moral of the story is that blended families do require explaining, but that's nothing to be afraid of. Whether we are correcting people who call us by the wrong last name or trying to draw our family tree, we try to make sure our families make sense to the people around us. Explanation is communication, and communication fosters understanding. Understanding is our key to a world in which all kinds of families are accepted and supported.

The answer to the quiz question is C. Having different last names is becoming very common, and most of us are quite able to deal with the minor complications without too much fuss. We usually view our own families as normal.

Stepparents Under Scrutiny

▼ ▼ ▼ ▼ ▼ ▼ ▼ ▼ ▼ ▼ ▼ ▼ ▼ ▼ ▼ ▼ ▼ ▼

Quiz Question

True or False: We will automatically dislike stepparents simply because they are stepparents.

▼ ▼ ▼ ▼ ▼ ▼ ▼ ▼ ▼ ▼ ▼ ▼ ▼ ▼ ▼ ▼ ▼ ▼

(Answer to quiz at end of section)

So far we have discussed many of the challenges facing blended families. Now we want to ask, how do our relationships with stepparents look after meeting those initial challenges? What do we have to say after the dust has settled? Here is a collection of descriptions, a peek into the way we honestly view our relationships.

Stewart's stepfather really took over the dad duties for Stewart when he was a small child. "When I was younger my stepdad used to go to Indian Guides with me, which is a father-son outdoor club. Indian Guides is like Boy Scouts, but you go to the meetings with your dad. We wore little leather vests that had patches on them for all the things we'd done. We told stories and ate cookies and went on little camp-outs. My stepdad and I liked doing outdoor things. He is a mountain man, he is Paul Bunyan, he can do anything physical. And he is always fixing things. When I got older, I would help him fix things around the house. My mom and my stepdad taught me discipline and learning through responsibility, and so if my car broke down, he'd help me fix it. I grew to appreciate him because of things like that. I am sure at first my mom would say to him, 'Stewart was wondering if you'd like to do this,' and he wanted to do it to get the marriage off to a good start. When a new person takes the role of the father, usually the kids don't want him. At least that's how it happens in the movies, and that's the only model I've got. You have to play baseball with them, and win them over. It just comes with the territory." Stewart's story points out the importance of becoming a child's friend—and really enjoying the activity.

Each blended family is different, with different needs, but being a friend is a strategy that will probably never fail. Hazel's relationship with her stepmother never took on a parental spin. "We have a really good relationship. She is like a sister to me. She never tried to be a mom, and it really worked out well. We were always friendly, and I did not feel threatened by her, like some people say they feel about stepparents." Alex also found a successful way to relate to his stepmother: "I just treated Melanie like I would a friend of my dad's. I still do. She's a cool woman, probably way better than my dad deserves! I have a good relationship with her now."

Greg describes how his stepmother-to-be became his ally after their first meeting: "I first met her when I was sixteen. My dad wanted me to meet her when I was visiting him one time. I didn't really understand the significance of it; he just said he wanted me to meet someone, and I guess I was too young to know what *someone* meant when a grown-up says it that way. She is extremely different from my mom. My mom is quiet, modest, and very nice. Bridget is nice, too, but much more gregarious and loud. She's almost my mother's polar opposite. My feeling before getting to know her was that I didn't really think that she belonged in my life. I was not sure if she belonged in my father's life either. I had a hard time accepting the idea of her being a part of my life because I felt like I was betraying my mom. I remember noticing when I met her that she smoked pretty heavily. I was really surprised because I made my dad quit when I was thirteen. When I was sixteen and I was smoking, it didn't look good for me to do it around him. One of the first things my stepmother did was offer me a cigarette, and of course I took one because I felt like the balance was in my favor. So that made me feel a little more comfortable with her." Greg did struggle with the idea of having a stepparent, but as happens to most of us, once he got to know his stepmother, he was able to form an opinion about her independently of her stepparent status. Our personalities are what matter.

Older kids feel more at ease when stepparents relate to them as adults. Martin enjoys spending time with his soon-to-be stepfather because of their common interests. "He treats me fine! We get along. He takes a really strong interest in what I do. He was a biochemistry major, like me, and I think he's really thrilled about that area. Of course, because our interests are so similar, I think he lives vicariously through me sometimes. He really enjoys talking to me about what he does with his lab and finding out what my classes are like. We talk about a lot of different stuff." Martin found that his mother and stepfather made a good team. "Effectively, talking to my mom or stepfather is really the same thing. They both talk to each other all the time. So if I tell my mom something she'll tell my stepfather, too. I can talk to him about it and see what he thinks." Martin's stepfather opened the lines of communication in his family, which brings them closer together.

Lawrence remembers some mixed feelings about his father's remarriage because his father had an affair with his stepmother prior to his parents' divorce. Lawrence talked about being with his father and stepmother now. "I've spent a lot of time with them. Whenever my siblings and I saw my father, she was often there. She's a really nice lady. She's very kind. She's tough. We all recognized that it would be very good for my father to have a tough woman around to keep him in line. I was upset, as I think we all were, when we found out that he was actually going to marry her, because she had been the symbol of the collapse of the marriage. But at the same time, I've never had any personal feelings against her or any reason to dislike her." As we grow older, we are able to relate to our stepparents based on who they are instead of on their symbolic status in our family. Some of us forge bonds so strong that they outlast our parent's relationships with their partners! Ben retains affection and respect for his former stepfather after his mother's second divorce: "I love him. I have to credit him with a lot of raising me. There was a period of time where I didn't see my father that much, and I saw Luigi a lot. I think he's a great guy. We got along very well. I have always looked at him as some sort of father."

Like Ben, Denise was very young when her parents split, and her stepmom cared for her a lot. "I lived with my mom and saw my dad and stepmom on the weekends. My stepmom took care of me a lot; she didn't have kids, so she didn't have anybody else taking her attention. My mom had a really small family, so when people needed to take care of me it was always my dad's family. We were really close. I always called my stepmom by her first name; I never called her Mom, but we were really affectionate." Denise and her stepmother went through some rough waters as their family dealt with moves, adolescence, and other turmoils. But now they are friends again. "In my sophomore year of college, when I came home for Christmas my stepmom and I were up drinking until 5:30 in the morning on Christmas Eve. We had a night of getting it all out. She is wonderful. I said what I'd lied about while growing up, all the secrets I'd kept so that no one would get upset. We talked about my parents; we talked about the relationship that the two of us had, and about our family's history. It was a huge, huge deal. We're very close."

For Lydia, who didn't meet her father or her stepmother until she was seventeen, the transition into a new family was very difficult. She at first felt that her stepmother was intrusive and tried to control her relationship with her father. Lydia said, "I think she picked up on my feelings after a while. She finally got a grip. She apologized to me and said, 'I've known your father for so much longer then you have.' And I said, 'That's great. Give me a chance to know him before you jump down my throat about the things you think I should be doing.' And that was it. We've never talked about it since. She and I are close now. We're friendly and sweet to each other. I really do like her. I think she's good for my dad, but every once in a while she starts telling me what she thinks I should do. She wants me to get to know my dad, but she wants me to know him the way she knows him, and that's not what I want." Lydia reminds us that even though we may not always be able to agree with our stepparents, we can still maintain a friendly relationship.

Sometimes our disagreements are so large, or our personalities so different, that we just aren't able to be friends. Mark told us he didn't get along very well with his former stepmother. "I think she was just a cold person. She was really anal about keeping things clean and making sure that I would do a bunch of chores. She wasn't so nice, but for the sake of my dad I tried to get along with her. We had conflict all the time, though. Especially when she was trying to have authority over me, I always resisted. From the time I was able to have opinions, I would say to her, 'I really think my dad should leave you.' Eventually my dad did leave her, and he keeps saying he wishes he had listened to me sooner. He got remarried and, thankfully, my new stepmother and I are friends."

Comments about liking stepparents because they like our parents were common with the people we interviewed. It is not surprising: many of us have seen our parents go through the heartache of divorce, and we are glad to see them happy again. Meredith describes what it feels like to live with her stepfather: "It's like having a really dorky older brother. If it wasn't for the fact that he and my mom sleep together, it would be exactly like that. There is just this really funny guy living in my house who does all the computer stuff. My feeling is that a husband's main job is to make sure he is a good husband, and the only judge of that is the wife. If my mom likes him and he makes her happy, that's all I care about. I wouldn't choose him, but she probably wouldn't want to live with whoever I chose, either. I care about him, but it's a reflected love; Mom loves him, and I love her, so therefore, by reflection, I love him."

Laura also has a stepfather, and she is glad her mother remarried. "I never acted out because of that marriage. I really liked my stepdad, and he wasn't at all intrusive; he didn't try to be my dad, but he took an interest in my life. He did not discipline me but totally supported my mom; he was present, but he was not controlling. It couldn't have been more perfect because my mom had somebody to talk to, yet I didn't have somebody trying to be my dad. I love my stepdad; I hug him when I see him, I talk to him when I call, and when I have had crises over the past few years, my stepdad has been welcome to join in the consoling and advice giving."

The relationships we discuss here cover a range of feeling; they go from rather cold to warm and supportive. All of the relationships went through a period of transition, and the healthy ones that made it through were based on trust between the stepparent and stepchild. How do you build that trust? Children want to know that stepparents are interested in them for who they are and are ready to listen to their concerns. It is worth repeating that these descriptions are from a small sample, and there are many others whose relationships are characterized by more antagonism, neglect, or even dislike. But with these slices of blended family life, we wanted to show that it really is possible for stepchildren to regard their stepparents with esteem and affection. All it takes is a little respect, friendliness, and effort— well, maybe a lot.

The answer to the quiz question is False. We all have different relationships with our stepparents. What matters is how we treat one another.

Will My Real Parents Please Stand Up?

▼ ▼ ▼ ▼ ▼ ▼ ▼ ▼ ▼ ▼ ▼ ▼ ▼ ▼ ▼ ▼ ▼ ▼ ▼

Quiz Question

Building trust and loyalty with your stepchildren requires:
   a. Time together and an honest, friendly atmosphere
   b. A written set of rules
   c. A lot of candy
   d. Belittling their other family

▼ ▼ ▼ ▼ ▼ ▼ ▼ ▼ ▼ ▼ ▼ ▼ ▼ ▼ ▼ ▼ ▼ ▼ ▼

(Answer to quiz at end of section)

Loyalty must build up over time. Since children in blended families divide their time, do they also divide their loyalties? The answer is usually yes, and that fact can be hard to live with. A stepfather who cares for his stepchildren on a daily basis may resent their loyalty to their biological father, whom they see less often. Or the reverse may be the case: a biological parent may feel threatened by a child's closeness to her stepparent. Once again these situations put the children in the middle—in a "twin gravity pull" between the people who care about them. Being devoted to both sides of a blended family is not hard in itself, but it becomes hard when parents and stepparents try to prevent us from acknowledging our multiple loyalties. Children of blended families need to be given the freedom to recognize and love all the people they are close to, all the time. We cannot shut off our emotions just by walking in a different front door.

These first few stories are about meeting a biological parent for the first time. Some children did not experience the "traveling between two homes" aspect of a blended family. They grew up in one home, never knowing one of their parents or that parent's new family. Loyalty needs time to grow, and without time, these people initially felt little loyalty to their birth parents. It is more proof that the people we view and treasure as our families are those who cared for us as children and treat us well, not necessarily those with whom we share genetic information. Loyalty must be earned.

Derek's father and mother divorced the day before he was born. His grandfather was like a dad to him, but he died when Derek was young. Then Derek's mother remarried, and he was hopeful about finally having a father, but that marriage ended soon after. These events solidified Derek's close bond with his mother, but they effectively ruined his faith in fatherhood. Derek decided to meet his biological father for the first time when he was eighteen because he wanted some information about his past, but that one meeting was all he wanted. He told us, "My father has been married three times in my lifetime, and he's had kids in every marriage. When we planned to meet for the first time, he offered to bring his kids along. I told him, 'I don't want to meet your kids; I'm not interested in that. I just want to talk to you.' Since then he's sent me a couple of e-mails, inviting me to have dinner or something. But I feel absolutely no obligation to try to ease any guilt that he might feel by spending time with him. I got what I needed out of it, so I don't think I'll ever see him again. I decided that I don't want to ever have a father again, because I feel like if I did, it would just fail, and I don't want to go through the stress of that. I remember when I was thirteen my mother made a pact with me that she would never get married again." Derek's story is sobering but understandable, since his father had never been a part of his life. It is valuable because it reminds us that regular caring and being there for one another are what builds families.

Nina had a similar situation, except that now she has spent time establishing ties with her father and stepmother. "The first time we met I felt very uncomfortable because he just kept looking at me. I understand that he could not believe what he was seeing, since he hadn't seen me in seventeen years, but I'm sure my face was red the entire three hours that we talked. He cried and cried, and I was so emotionless that I felt bad. At the time he was just a man I had never known, so meeting him wasn't something that had an effect on me. I just thought, 'Okay, it's time to get to know the other half of who I am.' But he came down to visit a lot, and now we're beyond getting to know each other, and he's my dad. We get along, and he treats me like he's always known me. He has answered a lot of questions that I had, and he's really straightforward about his life. That makes me have more respect for him than I had in the beginning. I think he's pretty cool. For the first four or five months I didn't know his wife. I'd talk to her on the phone, and she'd tell me that she loved me, and I was evasive, just saying, 'Can I talk to my dad?' Now I know Mary and she is wonderful. She's always happy and always loud. She's one of those people who I don't think ever had a bad day in her entire life." Nina's story has a happy ending precisely because she and her father invested the time to build a relationship.

For those of us who have known both of our parents all along, loyalty remains a critical issue. Children who have seen their parents get a divorce realize that those two people don't wish to be involved in each others' lives; yet because of us, they are. We would like to see them get along, for our sake, because it removes some of the strain of being the connecting link between parties that don't want to be connected, and because it is the easiest way for us to deal with our feelings of loyalty to both. But our families don't always do what we want(!), and so we are left juggling several people's time and feelings, trying to please, trying to figure out who can be trusted, trying to determine where we stand.

Denise told us about a conflict between her mom and stepmother that revolved around her. "My stepmom sometimes criticized my mom. I think she felt that I wasn't taken care of because I would arrive at my dad's house with my clothes packed in a grocery bag. I packed my own bag beginning when I was only four, so I'd forget underwear or I'd forget my homework or some other basic necessity. My mom cared, but she has never been the kind of mom who is always saying, 'Let's make sure that everything is under control.' So I think my stepmom was upset about that. She would always disagree with whatever my mom said or did."

When Denise's mom decided they would move two thousand miles away from Denise's dad, things really heated up. "When I moved it was horrible. My mom just said to my dad one day in passing, 'Oh, by the way, we are moving across the country,' instead of, 'Let's sit down and talk about what is going to happen,' like normal, mature people do. My dad was devastated. He was going to lose his only child. My dad's family was also really upset that I was leaving because I was the only grandchild that lived in the state. They had all taken care of me when I was growing up and were very attached to me. I remember one day I was in the car with my stepmom, and she was telling me that I didn't love my dad, that I didn't have any respect for my family, that I was doing the wrong thing by moving with my mom. I was twelve years old; I was doing what my mom said I was going to do! It was horrible, and I didn't like my stepmom for quite a while. Everybody in my dad's family was critical of my mom, and I was really protective of her. We spent a lot of time alone together because she didn't have many friends. I should not have had to defend my mom, but I was one hundred percent with her. It took me a long time to get over being very upset by the whole incident." Denise was deeply hurt when her stepmother suggested that she wasn't being loyal to them. Clearly Denise's father and stepmother were deeply hurt themselves that they had not been warned about the move, but instead of discussing their feelings, they put Denise in an agonizing position. It is not wrong for a child to love both sides of her family, and she will breathe easier knowing that both her parents respect that.

When Tanya went to visit her father, it was her stepmother who looked after her. "When I went to visit them, she would have time off from work, so I spent most of my time with her. She would take me places: to see my relatives, to the water slides with my half brothers. She was really the one being the parent. She thought it was really cute to have a daughter. She always came up with fun things for us to do; that is what she's good at doing. My dad's idea of taking care of the kids, from what I can tell, is watching hockey and ordering pizzas. My stepmom's ideas were like, 'Let's have a neighborhood party! We'll have a scavenger hunt for all the kids, and then they can come over and jump on our trampoline, and we'll make a cake . . . ' We're talking fun. Plus, she always listened to me." Now Tanya's stepmother and father are getting a divorce, and she is being penalized for her loyalty to the stepmother who cared so much for her. Her father and his relatives will not speak to her because she remains close to her father's former wife. Again, it is not hard to see that Tanya's father must be feeling threatened by the rapport Tanya has built with her stepmother, but he has not chosen the right way to deal with his feelings. Instead of facing them and talking about them, he has pushed Tanya into a no-win situation: lose her father or lose her stepmother.

Not all loyalty battles are so epic; some are much smaller and yet just as symbolic. Nora remembers a fight about the night of her college graduation: "I remember my mom and I had a fight that lasted for a couple of days about the fact that my dad was going take me to dinner on the night of graduation. She was really mad about it. She said that she and my stepdad were the ones who had supported me, put me through college, and how could I be such an ungrateful traitor as to go to dinner with my father on this big night. To me the whole ceremony and dinner didn't mean much, but to her it apparently did." There may be no solution to such problems that pleases everyone; compromise is an important skill. It might have helped Nora's family to discuss her graduation together, so that she understood how important it was to her mother before making a decision to be with her father. She may still have ended up hurting one of her parent's feelings, but hopefully less than she did by making a decision without knowing how her mother felt.

Some loyalty disputes are not actually overt enough to be called battles; perhaps they are more aptly named loyalty campaigns. A loyalty campaign takes place when parents and stepparents do not actually verbalize their complaints and yet manage to make their attitudes known. Allison told just such a story: "My dad was very condescending to me. He seemed to be saying, 'Yeah, your mom's crazy. We just let you go over there because we think that it is important for you to see her, but we're the responsible ones; we are the smart ones; we are the actual parents. She's just this crazy lady that you visit sometimes.' I think that attitude is probably the most damaging of all of the slander that I heard from them. They were not saying something that I, as a child, could see was false. If someone says, 'Your mom is stupid,' you can think, 'Is she stupid? You know, I don't actually think she is stupid.' But this was, 'Go with your mom. If you feel nervous, just call me. If she feeds you nothing but lentils for more than three days in a row, call me; if she just wanders off and you can't find her, don't worry, you've got a responsible parent back here.' You can't really argue with that. When you are seven or ten, you can't articulate how that makes you feel. You can't sit down and say, 'You are wrong about her, and you are wrong for telling me this.' All you can do is wonder, 'Is my mom on probation from parenting?' My dad used to say all the time that he was the 'custodial parent.' I thought for years that this was a legal term. The way he said it was, 'I make the decisions. I am the smart one. I am the reasonable one. I am the custodial parent.' I was so angry when I found out that all that meant was that he got to have us more often. I told him, 'It doesn't mean that you are a better parent; it just means you had a better lawyer, you idiot.'" These attitudes and insinuations fit under the heading "Trying to Turn Your Child Against Her Other Parent" in the unwritten Book of Parental No-No's, and they are not a good way to earn a child's trust. They are manipulative and puerile, and eventually the child will grow up and realize that she has been misled by her biased parent. The parent will not have communicated anything but sour grapes.

When we are not being pulled in opposite directions by our loyalties, we can find ourselves feeling pushed away. Allison, whose stepmother has had an active parenting role in her life, also told us about a time when she felt left out of her stepmother's devotions: "My stepmother has a sister and an aunt in France. One time about a year ago she was talking about going out there to visit, and she said, 'Oh, the kids should go,' meaning my two little half siblings. 'That would be great; they could finally meet their family.' And I said, 'Why wouldn't Janet (my sister) and I go? The kids are only three and five; they won't care about France. Janet and I want to go. We want to meet the family.' She said, 'But they're not your family.' And all of a sudden I had this massive brain attack. It just dawned on me, 'Ohhhh, well, you can take your flesh-and-blood children there, but we are just the paper children, the ones you are only technically related to!' Janet and I were both pretty offended by the whole thing; it has never really been resolved. Finally nobody went, but it was a major break. The whole time we were growing up she had said, 'You are just as much my kids as they are; you don't have to worry about that. There is no difference; you are my daughters too.' She would always say, 'I didn't just marry your father; I married all three of you.' But after that it was like, 'Wow, I guess not.'" This story is about the difficulty with which true bonds get established, and how easily they are damaged by carelessness and insensitivity.

We develop commitments to the people who care for us, who show interest in us, and who love us. Those people are not always our biological parents, a fact which can be difficult for others to understand. Kara grew up with her stepfather, to whom she is very close; she only occasionally visited her father. It is clear in her mind who her 'dad' is and who will therefore get the corresponding privileges. It is not clear for everyone else, however. She told us, "When I get married someday, my stepfather will walk me down the aisle, I am sure of that. Anyway, my father has other girls. Every few years, my stepmother will say, 'You know, when you get married, just have them both walk you down the aisle, then there won't be any confusion.' I'm thinking, 'No confusion? I think that's really confusing.'" It's the same lesson: genes do not make up for time spent together.

In reading these stories, we may wonder how parents can do or say such awful things to their sons and daughters. We must remember that the transitions blended families go through evoke very strong emotions. When people are feeling hurt, abandoned, jealous, or threatened, they sometimes say spiteful or unkind things to other people, including their children. Because blended families generally go through more such turbulent transitions, they are susceptible to these very human forces. If we are to close the gaps between blended families and two-biological-parent families, this may be where we need to start. There is no simple three-step plan for expressing and dealing positively with emotions as a family, but it must be done somehow. When we are communicating with one another, we are less likely to misunderstand one another. That will not make negative feelings disappear, but it will help children know that they are not at fault. Vanessa recounted one incident in which cooperation made all the difference: "All three of my parents——my dad, my mom, and my stepdad—drove me up to school when I started college. I was struck by how much my family works together when I saw my dad and my stepdad assembling my bed together. They were truly amiable, and it made me thankful to be in a family where people respect one another. It meant that they were concentrating on supporting me, not competing with each other. We even went out to dinner as a group."

Loyalty battles are miserable, and children of blended families should not be coerced into favoring one part of their family over another. Parents often feel that they, and not their former spouse, are the logical choice for their children's love. But our loyalty grows with time and experience; it is not simply dammed and channeled in any direction. We know we do not always do exactly what our parents would wish, but their dissatisfaction is not our cross to bear, and when it is forced upon us, we are hurt by it. If facing their own emotions can help parents and stepparents protect their children from growing up with stories like some of those in this section, then it is a small price to pay. If one of our parents does not deserve our loyalty, we will discover that on our own. No matter which part of our family we might be with, we need the freedom to be honest about who we love.

The answer to the quiz question is A. Loyalty and trust cannot be bought or coerced into being. There is no substitute for time spent together; it is the best foundation on which to build relationships.

Part Three

Looking Back

This is the most important fact about children, all children: they grow up. Childhood is an important time in any human's life, but the fact is, we spend most of our lives as adults. The implication of these obvious facts is that since we spend more time remembering our childhoods than living them, it matters how we view them in retrospect. Our goal has been to show that children of blended families can grow up to be just as successful, mature, and self-reliant as anyone else, and now it is time to let our interviewees speak as adults.

We asked our peers about their present lives, their views of the past now that they are grown, and the nature of their relationships with their families. Our story would not be complete without these remarks because children do not exist in a vacuum: the goal of raising a child is to introduce a strong, wise, kind human being into the world. Clearly children are wonderful in and of themselves, but there is not a parent alive who doesn't have one eye on the future, wondering what his or her daughter or son will grow up to be. We all make many decisions in our lives we will not know the merit of until some time in the future. Did I pick the right school? job? house? That is just the way life is. But what could be more important than decisions affecting one's child? And what could be more strenuous that waiting eighteen, maybe twenty, years to see the results?

We want to reassure blended families by sharing our experiences. Here is the final chapter. For blended families today, here is a telescope into the future. Our focus will be first on how our stepparents earned our respect, how they learned to fit into our lives. Then we turn back to ourselves and discuss how we dealt with the rigors of blended family life. This is important because no one just skates through events such as divorce and remarriage. They require deliberate adjustment and effort, and these experiences play a central role in shaping our personalities. We asked our interviewees to talk about their current relationships with their parents, stepparents, and siblings, and then, perhaps most important, we asked them for their advice. No family is perfect; we all have some room for improvement. Listen to their words of experience, humor, and honesty, and notice that what it boils down to is, "Take it easy. It's going to be okay." These are true stories, and they are stories of triumph, hope, and love.

R-E-S-P-E-C-T: Find Out What It Means

As is probably clear by now, relationships between new blended family members have something important in common with all human relationships: we like people who are kind to us, who listen well, who are friendly and respectful. Our interviewees discussed how their stepparents earned their respect—and the ways are innumerable. Stepparents must be sensitive and pay attention to what each individual child needs. Some need a game of baseball, some need a wise listening ear, and some just need a bit of distance.

Suzanne's stepfather made the right moves from the very beginning. She told us, "I really liked Craig when I first met him. He didn't try to come in and take over. It wasn't like, 'I'm your mom's new husband, so you better listen to what I say.' It wasn't anything like that. It was 'Hi, I'm Craig. Nice to meet you. I've heard a lot about you.' He was a good guy. Even in a problem situation, he'll listen to my side first, asking, 'What's going on for you? Why did this happen? Tell me the whole story.' And that's way better for me then saying, 'This is what I heard. This is what I saw. You're grounded.' I know parents who do that. It is very irritating." Suzanne told us another story showing that her stepfather's patience and willingness to listen have made a lasting impression on her. "It was the middle of my senior year. I didn't know what I wanted to do. I didn't want to go to a big university; I was flipping out. And he said, 'Write down all the things you want to do in your lifetime.' I wrote: 'therapy school, go on to become a therapist, et cetera.' Then he said, 'Pick one now.' And he helped me find a school and do what was necessary to get into that school, instead of saying, 'You don't know what you want to do? God, everyone knows what they want to do.' It's the listening skills. If you don't know how to use them, then you're not going to be a good parent."

Ben told us about when he would have appreciated a little more sensitivity on his stepfather's part: "This seems sort of trivial, but it isn't trivial at all. When Luigi discusses something, he gets very, very passionate about it. I have seen him and his friends discussing things—they're yelling at each other like crazy and they are really excited. On a few occasions I got into arguments with him, and I just couldn't handle it. I would always burst into tears. He was so, so forceful in the way he spoke. It didn't have to do with me, that's just the way he was. He came up and apologized to me afterward, and it was okay. We just have different personality types. I'm rather sensitive, and he's got an assertive manner." Luigi's apology for unintentionally hurting Ben's feelings allowed them to maintain a close relationship.

Needless to say, people are different and react to the same situation in diverse ways, as Ben's story shows. That is even true within the same family, as Stewart told us. "You have to play it by ear. Some kids are going to take everything, including you, completely differently than others. My brother and I are two perfect examples. My brother was older when our father died, so he felt that he had a father and that his father was taken away from him. He felt shortchanged by life, like he was never going to have a father again, so he wanted no part of it when my stepfather became part of our family. That made my brother grow stronger, but more closed emotionally than I think he should be. I was affected that way a bit, but also I felt lucky because I was given another chance to have a dad. I felt I had two fathers." Stewart's stepfather had a difficult job, but by listening to his stepsons' requests for attention or space, he did what was best for each of them.

Lawrence had an interesting story about how his stepmother earned his respect: "My stepmother is very open and straightforward, and she said at the beginning that she really liked my mother and respected the job she had done raising us. That was really nice to hear. She thought my dad was the delinquent one in many ways! And she would also relay messages to my mother through a mutual friend about things related to the family. Once when she and my dad were fighting quite a bit, Claire, my stepmother, didn't think it was a good idea to have my younger brother around. And so she relayed a message to my mother saying she didn't think their home was a good place for my brother to be—because they were fighting, not because she didn't want my brother there. My mother did what she could to get my brother away from that. I think Claire did a good job because she was nice and kind, but also frank, open, and talkative. And she didn't get involved in my life. I would have resented that because that's not her place. But I was a teenager; for younger kids it would have been a different story." These are the kind of little things that make us feel our stepparents really care about what is best for us.

Unfortunately, some people don't seem to have any interest in creating a relationship with their stepchildren, which is sure to arrest the process. Martin told us about his difficulties with his stepmother: "She and I never actually talked one-on-one, by ourselves, without my dad being there. She showed no desire to get to know me as a person, or to do things with me without my father there. I never got the impression that she was really the least bit interested in me as a person or as her potential stepson. If she had been more friendly and interested in what I was doing, maybe tried to be a little bit more active in my life and show me that it was okay to get to know her, then our relationship would have been a lot better. I was too young at the beginning to have any feelings of dislike for her from thinking, 'This is the woman who stole my father away from my mom.' I developed those feelings over time because of the way she originally treated me. I think that she could have prevented that if she had taken a more active role in my life and tried to be more of a positive figure instead of a negative one." What else can be said?

Little can match the pain of indifference, but the indignity of disrespect is also hard to bear. Nora had this to say to new stepparents: "From the very beginning my stepfather was really big on respect. But he lacked the ability to see that you don't just get it because you're a parent or a step-in parent. You have to earn it. It seems like a pretty simple equation, but it's hard to remember. A child is a person, no matter what age. Kids are thinking, and they are pretty aware of what's going on. You have to have a lot of respect for who they are and not just pander to them. Listen to what they are saying, and rethink what you are saying. Treat them almost as an adult as much as you can."

When our stepparents are friendly and open, we may become very close. Tanya has maintained a relationship with her stepmother even as her ties with her father have suffered, and it is not hard to see why. Tanya told us, "My stepmom has always been sweet. In fact, I'm waiting for a phone call from her right now. She invited me to come spend time with her and my brothers this summer. She is going to pay for part of my flight. And my dad will not be involved with it." Like many others, Tanya places her loyalty with the one who has shown she cares.

But family bonds are not a win-lose game. Rebecca's stepmother was a positive influence in her life by helping her connect with her father: "I think my stepmother is kind of a mitigating factor on my dad. He is a sort of distant, stiff kind of person; I mean, he is very sweet, but it's hard for him to talk about his feelings in a spontaneous way. My stepmother is much better at that kind of thing, and she played the go-between for my dad and me when I was a teenager and we were having trouble. She'd say to me, 'Your dad feels this way.' And I would tell her what I thought. Then she would go and tell him, and it was helpful. It might have been nicer if my dad and I could have talked to each other face-to-face, but she made our lives much easier."

There is one scenario that we have failed to mention so far, and that is when children do not accept a stepparent's attempts at becoming friends. There are probably also circumstances in which neither party desires a relationship and so both are content with remaining distant. But perhaps nothing is more difficult for a newcomer than trying to build a relationship with a stepchild who won't meet him or her halfway. Older children may benefit from an honest conversation in which they are allowed to voice their needs and wants and to hear those of their stepparents. But that may not be possible with younger children, who may just show their discontent by acting out. If the problem is serious and is disrupting the family, do not hesitate to seek help. Sometimes we need others to give us an outside perspective. And it probably wouldn't hurt to follow Lucy's advice: "I would advise the stepparent to back off. I think families are pretty delicate. Upsetting the old balance should be done very slowly or bad things will happen. It's pretty hard, especially for older kids and stepparents, to get along at all. I think the only way to do it is for the stepparent to go really slowly and not try to have too much input at the beginning."

Having said all that, we remember that no two families are alike. The most important theme to draw from these stories is that most of us appreciate friendliness, but some need time alone. We are usually more comfortable when stepparents support rather than invade our lives, but some need extra attention. Concentrate on your own family. Each person is different, and the best way to find out what kind of interaction a stepchild needs is to ask. Simply by asking, you will initiate an atmosphere of mutual respect.

How We Coped

The people we talked to are articulate, well-adjusted young adults who are studying, working, and succeeding. How did we defy the statistics that predict our higher risk for jail sentences, teenage pregnancy, and failing grades? Like many other children of blended families, we found ways to cope with the changes that kept us afloat and flexible. Sometimes we went outside our families for help, sometimes we just looked inside ourselves for comfort. Divorce, remarriage, and the other transitions a blended family goes through can shake up our lives to a breaking point. Here is how we coped with the chaos.

Many of us work through our family's transitions by going outside our family for help. We can be comforted by the knowledge that we are not alone, that other children are dealing with the same issues we are. Martin found that talking to a friend who had a similar situation helped him cope with the strain in his family. "When I was in junior high school I started becoming a little bit more aware of what was happening in my family. I had a friend, who I'm still really good friends with, whose parents also got divorced when she was in seventh grade. We talked about it with each other a lot. It became easier for both of us to understand it by talking about it with each other. We both came to terms with what exactly had happened. Until I met her, I really didn't have any friends whose parents had gotten divorced. It was kind of rough being the only kid that I knew whose parents were divorced. I didn't really make it public knowledge. I never said, 'Hey, look what happened to me today. My parents got divorced.' It wasn't like that at all. It took a lot of getting used to, and talking with Leah helped."

Instead of talking to just a close friend, some of us find that talking to anyone at all can help us weather the storm. Jean-Luc found more than one outlet for his sadness: "I remember feeling like 'Here I am, another kid from a divorced family.' I felt very sad for a while. I had heard somewhere that if you told people about it and didn't keep it all clamped up inside, you'd feel better. So I told everyone. I made a point of it. If I just happened to be talking to someone obscure or who I didn't know very well, I would tell them. I think it really helped. I remember there was this one prayer that I always thought was funny. So one thing I'd do to cheer myself up is I would say this prayer with a silly accent. That would just crack me up to no end and I'd feel better." Even if we don't have one particular confidante, or a good joke, remembering the fact that there are many other families like ours can help us feel more at ease about our situations. Alex remembered understanding that he wasn't alone: "After a certain point I realized that there are so many families that are messed up, I just got used to it. It wasn't a big deal to me. I didn't feel that there was much I needed to do about it. And there was probably nothing I could do about it, so trying to remedy it was not worth my energy." It is important for us to be able to accept our families the way they are, even if they are confusing.

When our own family was adjusting to our mother's remarriage, we found that having a neutral third party mediate for us helped us to communicate honestly. Vanessa remembers: "At first I was nervous about seeing a family therapist, especially because my mom, dad, and stepdad would all be there together. Everyone seems to think that if you see a therapist, there is something terribly wrong with you. But it was very good for us to be able to talk about what was going on in our family in a low-pressure environment. I think it helped all of us understand more of how our family works, and it let us have our feelings in a safe place."

Some of us find that we are prone to deal with the changes in our families by withdrawing from other people and taking time out to be alone. Lawrence regrets not being more open with his siblings about his feelings, because his sister thought his distance meant that he didn't care. He told us, "My parents told me about everything that was going on long before they told my brother and sister, so I had already dealt with it to the extent that I could. I was in a position with my brother and sister where I was being the strong and tough one. I wasn't showing my emotions. Of course, the way my sister took it was, 'Oh, Lawrence is so emotionally aloof that this isn't bothering him at all. He's completely unlike me. I can't really relate to him.' That was too bad. I didn't find that out for a long time afterward. That was really a mistake on my part."

Jordan had a similar experience, also finding himself estranged from his sister, who was more vocal about her feelings: "She wanted to depend on me for support during that time. I hated the way that she dealt with it. We had very different mechanisms for dealing with the stress and pain of the situation. I would just instantly turn inward and not deal with it. I would block everything out and read. Isabel would throw a fit and scream and cry. She would threaten to call the cops and run off to my aunt. She wanted me to come and support and comfort her. If I had done that, then I would have had to think about it. And I didn't want to. So I didn't help her, and that frustrated her, which frustrated me. She always says now, 'I came to you, and I wanted your help so much, and you just wouldn't open up to me.' I think, 'You couldn't understand the situation I was in, and how your intrusion into it would make the situation unbearable for me.' That was a strain on our relationship. We just didn't deal with it together. We were both in our separate little rooms."

Whether we scream and cry or sit and sulk, we are trying to come to terms with how our families are changing. Most of us do come to terms with it, and soon after we may forget that we thought it was strange in the first place. The vast majority of us regard our families as completely normal, even with their complexities. Hazel's family has a long history of rocky marriages which has affected how her parents handled their own. However, she told us that she feels less dramatic about what she has gone through than the people she talks to about it: "When my grandmother and grandfather got divorced, my dad was five, and they carried on a charade until my dad was thirteen. He didn't know that his parents were divorced that whole time. You know, it's funny because when I talk to my dad about that, I'll say, 'My God, I can't believe it, you must be so mad.' He always says, 'It's no big deal.' And I think people are going to say the same thing to me when I tell them, 'My parents got divorced when I was two, they got back together, they had my sister, and they broke up again.' They say 'Wow. That must have been tough on you.' And I'm thinking, 'No, not really.'" People can be tougher and more resilient than we expect.

Our families are the standards to which we compare other experiences. Sometimes we don't even notice a certain trait about our family until we see something that mirrors or opposes it in the world around us. Jean-Luc figured out slowly that his parents weren't happy with each other, not long before his father left to marry another woman. "In retrospect, I guess I had a few clues to the fact that they didn't have a very happy marriage. One of them was that I had this girlfriend named Madison who had long red hair and was very cute. But we had absolutely nothing in common. Our conversations were always very tense and cold. I noticed that my parents used the same tone of voice to talk to each other as I used with Madison. I remember thinking, 'Gee, maybe there's something wrong here.' The other clue was that just before they got separated I went to stay at a different girlfriend's place. Her parents were married and actually were living in a relationship. You could really see them struggle and sometimes fight and make up. This was so strange to me. I had always assumed that marriage was just this functional role that people played. I started to realize that my parents didn't really have a relationship. I even remember trying to counsel my father once, saying, 'Dad, you should really take Mom out to the movies or something like that.'"

Like all children, as we grow to become adults, our independent identities take shape and we are able to reflect on the ways in which our families have affected us. Ben described how his experiences in a blended family have taught him lessons about commitment: "It's absolutely crucial to me that when there is a commitment made that it's stuck to. I know that's a result of the divorce. I just told myself in my brain a million times, 'If you ever make that promise to someone, make sure it's something that you are going to be able to keep. You hold to that commitment.' I think it's affected me in the relationships I've had because I do tend to make strong commitments that I keep."

Every child has her own way of getting through the obstacles and challenges her family presents. In general, we do need someone to talk to, but no one can force us to bare our feelings if we aren't ready. We ultimately decide what we will tell to whom, and whether or not we will communicate with our family or "check out" until the storm has passed. Most of us find that after some time we are able to accept our families for what they are, perfect or not.

We're Still Our Parents' Kids

After stories about traveling, holiday chaos, custody battles, new homes, and new names, probably some burning questions remain in your mind: What do these grown children think of their parents and stepparents now? What are their relationships like? Here we will answer those questions. The stories here further support one point we have tried to make all along, and that is that in many ways blended families are no different from other families. Some of them are close, some are good at communicating, and some are not. But whatever the case, the sensitivity, compassion, and strength with which these stories are told is cause for hope.

Parents need someone to look after them, too, and many of us are glad to have a stepparent who wants the job. Jay told us a particularly moving story about the difference his stepmother made in his, and his father's, life. "A little less then a year after they were married, my dad found out he had cancer. It's been really, really wonderful for her to be there for him and for us to have the financial stability that she is able to bring. I probably wouldn't have been in college this year if she hadn't been there for me. He was going through treatment my first semester, and there's no way I would have gone away to school if she weren't there the whole time with him. But she was, which was good!" Knowing that someone we love is being cared for is enough to endear our stepparents to us no matter what.

Zoe lived with her stepsister for a year, which gave her another reason to appreciate her stepmother. "My stepmother is very, very good at relationship stuff. She helped us to open up and talk, which is something that we didn't do growing up. I think she's basically the reason that Laurie, my stepsister, and I got through that year." We may not realize all that our stepparents do for us when we are young, but isn't that normal in parental relationships? Grown-up kids realize their gratitude.

Zoe is also grateful for the fact that she was able to remain close to both parents even when they didn't remain close to each other. She said, "I told my mom that my father made a comment to me that his relationship with Paula, my stepmother, was the first fully emotional relationship he's had. She got a sad, bittersweet expression in her eye; it was a 'That's really wonderful that he found love' look. When he came out to visit me at school, we had such a good time. I told her about it, and about some of the things that are going on in his life, because she doesn't know how he's doing or how his work is going. She's happy to hear that stuff, even though she wouldn't necessarily have a conversation with him herself."

Far from resenting her parents for their choices in life, Zoe is glad that they have finally found compatible companions. "My mom went out and bought a set of dishes for fifty people, intending to entertain all the time. That's one of the things she likes to do, and my stepfather is willing to do it with her. He's much more extroverted than my father. My father is a professor, and my stepmom's an attorney. They argue about economics for two hours, and it gets heated and they get upset. They go running off into the office to pick up books and look up their arguments. My parents are just very different. They make much more sense with the people they are with now. They are so much happier." Who wouldn't prefer to live with happy parents?

Ben grew up with his stepfather, but now his mother is divorced again. Ben confessed, "I've talked to my stepdad a couple of times. Because of the divorce it's been difficult for me to give him a call, even though I want to. That's a tough situation for me right now." But Ben has not forgotten how his stepfather influenced his life, in large ways and in small ones, too: "My chess game got a lot better. I learned a lot about music from him. I think I also started learning the art of conversation. He's really good at taking a subject and bringing up all the issues: 'Okay, I understand that point of view, but can you see it from this perceptive? And are you considering the side effect of this?' And I learned how to paint houses. He taught me a lot about what an artist's life is like, about being really passionate about your art form, just diving down and doing it, and losing yourself in it. It's really fascinating."

Ben also talked about getting to know his biological father: "My mom would tell me nasty stories about my dad when I was growing up. I think it gave me a really skewed image of my father. Gradually I learned that was not the whole picture, but as a kid, I thought my father was just a jerk. I was angry at him for a long time. I'm now getting over that; he isn't a total schmuck. My mom was upset at the time, so she told my sister and me about every single mistake my dad ever made. My own complaint about him is that he's constantly taking jobs that take him away from us. My view on that has changed, though, because when I was younger I felt that was something my dad did that was unforgivable. But now I understand his profession a little bit more, and I realize that sometimes you have to jump on every single bone that's tossed in your direction. Even if it means going to Venezuela for a couple of months." Ben reminds us of the fact that our parents are human, and they make mistakes. He loves his mother in spite of her anger towards his father, and he loves his father in spite of his absences.

As we get older, we learn to understand our parents as human beings just like us, and they do the same. Hazel told us, "My parents are very open and honest with me, sometimes to a fault. I think now that I am older, my parents feel that they can just speak to me like they would speak to anybody else; they tend to forget that their ex-spouse is actually my father or mother. My mom will mention that she thinks my dad is rather self-absorbed, for instance. But it never really offends me, because I lived with my dad for a long time, and I noticed that about him, too. My dad is just a real individual. He is an intuitive healer, but he also plays golf. He likes to read

Steinbeck, and he listens to Mahler and John Lennon, and he wears gas station pants. There is nobody quite like him. My mom and I both know that." That blended families demand more effort may not be such a bad thing after all. It allows us to get to know our parents in a unique way.

Having children grow up and leave the nest may be a particularly intense experience for single parents. Mark talked about how his mother has changed since he has left home: "She's acting like, 'Hell, no, I'm not getting remarried. I am a free woman!' Got rid of the pets; got rid of me—she doesn't *have* to do anything now. She loves it. She's totally in heaven. She is going to Australia for a month. Before she wouldn't leave me alone in the house, and now she'll take off for a few nights at a time. She would never do that before. She would never hop on a plane to go to another country, that's for sure. It's amazing." Mark's comments remind us that it is not only children who grow and change.

Mark, who was an only child, grew up visiting his dad's house every weekend. The scene in that home was constantly changing, and even though his father is currently remarried, Mark feels that he has always been the lowest common denominator, a point of stability, for his father. "My dad has had several wives. I've been the stable person in my dad's family. It's awesome. I think I make all of his wives jealous because I get more time with him than they do, which is the way I like it. My dad and I get a lot of time alone because I demand it. It's cool." His father's current wife is much younger, which has been fun for Mark. "Because we're so close in age, we have the same musical tastes. It was weird when I was listening to Morrisey or going to Clash concerts and she was into it, too! She lived in Minneapolis all her life, so she had a lot of gay friends, and we talk about the dating scene a lot, and it's cool. She's all right. I think it makes my dad more youthful. When I'm with my dad now, in his own old way, he's hip. He has the red car and the new wife; I think he's going for the ponytail—no, I hope he doesn't go for the ponytail." After a chuckle Mark continued, "My mom has met my half sister now. She's my only blood relative, and my mom realizes how important that is to me. My stepmother really likes me a lot, so she thinks my mom must have done something right in raising me. And so they all get along in this weird way. For me it's better than it's ever been."

Close relationships provide support that makes dealing with almost anything else, even pain, separation, and lawsuits, much easier. Lawrence said that of all his family, "I'm the closest to my mother by far. Throughout the divorce and all that followed, I think that my close friendship with my mom and her openness about the divorce made it easier in some ways. I felt I had some 'in' on what was going on."

Such a friendship with his father would have helped Martin, who has had trouble understanding his father's actions. "I guess my father felt that he needed to leave my mom because he was really in love with my stepmother, and I guess I understand, because I don't think that it would have been healthy for him to stay around and pretend that he was in love with my mom, just lying to her and to me and my sister. But I also feel that he could have saved us all a lot of hurt if he had just tried to get over whatever feelings he was having. The whole thing was just thrown at all of us. To this day, I struggle with why he decided to do what he did, but I guess he felt it was what he needed. If they had remained married, then maybe my life would have been a lot more emotionally stable, but on the other hand, because they got divorced I have met some wonderful people. My stepfather has been a far better father to me than my dad ever was. If they hadn't gotten divorced, I never would have met him."

Martin mentioned an issue that many people struggle with, and that is whether parents should stay married for their childrens' sake. This is clearly a question for a trained marriage counselor, but we can offer this: nearly everyone we interviewed believed their parents were better off divorced, despite the stress it brought. Erica adds, "Once I was talking with a close friend who asked me why my parents had gotten divorced. I had never thought about that question before. My mom and my dad have always seemed so different to me that I take it for granted that they shouldn't be married to each other." Children can sense a failed relationship; an unhappy marriage is hard to hide. If it's the right thing to do, we will understand.

Even when the divorce is inevitable, the transition can be sad for us if we are unable to start new relationships with our stepfamily, because it usually leaves us feeling estranged from our biological parents as well. Margarita watched her parents end their marriage, but she hasn't gotten the chance to become close to her stepfamily because she's never lived with them. She told us, "My parents got divorced and I moved out at nearly the same time, so it felt like one big change. My mom and her partner, Lynn, bought a house, and they didn't happen to have a room for me. Lynn, my sister, my brother, and my mom: that's really their family unit. There's a sense when I come back that it's something extra that upsets the balance of their house. In a way, I can't go home, because it's really just somebody else's home." But she is quick to describe the positive effects of leaving the nest early: "I feel pretty independent most of the time. I wouldn't say that it makes me feel unsettled, it just makes me feel like the place where I'm living by myself is my home. It's good because I've gotten away from that kind of unequal parental relationship with them. It makes me feel old more than anything." Early independence certainly may be one of the more beneficial side effects of growing up in a blended family, but it often comes at the cost of close relationships with our family members. Margarita's family could rebuild some intimacy with her by making an effort to make her feel included when she visited them.

Seth also sees his dad and stepmother only when he goes to visit. He told us, "I promised myself when I got my license and a car, the first thing I would do was go see my dad. And so I did. I got a truck, and I drove it up there, just by myself. I appreciate the fact that I am able to go see my dad whenever the heck I want, and I don't have to travel on that dumb, stinky bus. I told him, 'This is the way it's going to be from now on. I want to surprise you; I don't want to have to make an appointment with you. And if I show up on your doorstep, I expect you to take me in. You owe me that much. If I feel like being polite, I'll call before I come.' He loved it. He thinks it's the greatest thing in the world. The one thing he could ask from me is that I love him in return. And he knows this is the way I love." Seth is lucky that his father welcomes him on his terms.

Tanya wishes that she could patch things up with her father, whom she sees rarely. "I'm reading this book on anthropology, and I really want to go find some ruins in the desert this summer. And I was going to ask him to join me, because that's his favorite thing to do, so that we could go take a trip together and get closer. But now I can't do anything because I have to talk to his lawyer to get through to him. I will always be willing to forgive him, if he is ready to do it. But I don't think he is ever coming around, and I no longer see any point in putting any hope in it. I would be a daughter if he wanted me to be a daughter. But he doesn't want to be a dad." Tanya's father is fortunate to have a daughter who is so open and ready to forgive; the tragedy is that he doesn't know it. The loss that Tanya feels is enormous, because in many ways, she feels that she no longer has a father. Let it be a lesson to parents that their absence hurts us deeply when we are open to building a relationship with them.

In fairness, we should note that some of us don't mind seeing our parents only rarely. Suzanne summed up her relationship with her father in not so many words: "Since I moved out, he does his thing and I do my thing, and if we meet up, that's great, and if we don't, then that's fine too." No one guarantees that we will be close friends with our parents or children. Those who are close should remember that they are very lucky.

One way to increase the chances of having a friendly relationship is to talk. For many of us it's not easy, and it is often even worse for divorced parents and their respective spouses. A little encouragement may be in store. Abigail, before she left for college, took the initiative with her four parents. "I wrote them all a mean letter last year saying, 'I'm going to college, and you have to pay for it, so you better figure out how to talk to each other because I'm not going to be the go-between.' They tried to say that they are good, that they don't fight. But I said, 'No, you're not.' And they sort of mumbled sheepishly. They have been a lot more civil for the last year and a half."

Denise talked about how grateful she is that her parents can communicate: "My stepmom called my mom to talk about me while I was in college. I thought, 'Oh, God, they're communicating!' It was really wonderful for me. It was so nice to have two people concerned about me. I never had my whole family dealing with problems together because of having no siblings and having divorced parents. I was glad that my mom and my stepmom talked about their concerns together, because they could offer different perspectives, to each other and to me, like parents are supposed to do. They could support me together." Denise is very close to both her mother and her stepmom, whom she has known most of her life. She has put a lot of work into her relationships, and clearly it has paid off.

Jordan also lived with his stepfather for much of his childhood, but his mother is now redivorced. He has a very different story to tell. "It was a strange relationship. Paul had characteristics that were very admirable. He was a very hard worker; he was determined. He was incredibly strong. He was a wrestler in college, and his team actually won the NCAA championships. He was just a natural athlete. He could teach you a lot, and when you're fourteen, that's very important. So I admired him for his athletic prowess and his strength. He was generous at times. There were good things about him; he really wanted the best. I've never met anybody who tried so hard to do well in his life, to do the things that he knew were right. But he just couldn't. It was really painful watching both the struggle in Paul and in my mom trying to change him. She always had an eye for the good in people and wanted to bring it out. But you can't try to save somebody in a relationship, and eventually it just wore her out. She could not deal with it anymore. It's sad, but he wasn't going to change enough. He'd been severely abused as a kid, and he didn't have a lot of contact with his family. He was very aggressive and violent. He had a drug problem. I want a clean break from him. I've learned all I can learn from Paul; I've given all I can give. It gets to a point where you don't want to live in that sort of relationship any longer. It's not healthy for anybody. I did my time."

Jordan has reestablished contact with his father, but they have not yet met. "We're making slow, steady progress. And I'm going to go to Portugal to meet him and some of my other Portuguese family, to try to understand that part of the family." However, Jordan's interest in his father is difficult for his mother. "Because of their history and all she had to go through, it is hard for her that I want to meet him. It would be very painful for her if her son became close friends with the man who she sacrificed everything to get away from. She didn't even want me to see my Portuguese relatives. She actually forbade me from seeing them while I lived in her house. So I turned eighteen, moved out of her house, and saw them." Jordan's clarity of mind and strength regarding the trying circumstances of his past are remarkable. His insight proves that there are those who can rise above their pasts with grace and wisdom. Our purpose is to encourage others to do the same.

Being a parent takes practice, as do most things worth doing. Rebecca says that because both of her stepparents had not had children before, she felt like their test case. "I think they were both nervous. I feel really lucky with both my stepparents. Neither of them had kids before, and then they married somebody with a kid. I think for both of them it was a very positive experience to 'practice' on somebody else. They once told me that being a stepparent gave them courage about having their own kids." Although her two families lived on opposite sides of the country, they did not hesitate to come together for Rebecca. "I feel really lucky that when I was graduating from college they could all be there, all four of them. When I was getting married, everybody could be there, and nobody was tense. All the new spouses and their kids could be there, and everybody was fine with the others. They really did a good job of that."

Serena also has two stepparents to whom she is close. She said of her stepfather, "He is an easygoing, fantastic man. He talks slowly and is really intelligent. He is the kind of guy who is quiet more often than not, but when he says something, you know he has been listening to everything that's been going on and formulating a perfect gem of wit. And you look at him and crack up because he is so hilarious. He's also really hip, much more than my mom is. He's into the music scene in Austin, and so he knows a lot of the bands that I know. Sometimes it is amazing how much stuff he knows."

Serena's description of her stepmother is a bit different: "Lorraine is an L.A. woman, so whenever I need that, I call her and say, 'I need to go shopping.' And she's ready. She likes everything to match; she is always coordinated. Sometimes it gets on my nerves when I want to wear my old, sloppy, comfy clothes, but it's really great when I want to go out and get stuff for work. She figures out exactly what blazer I need, and which scarf will go with it. It is wonderful because my mom is always a little disheveled, like an English teacher. They are total opposites, and I can have whichever one I want. I have to look at it like that, as an opportunity, as opposed to some kind of curse."

A few years ago (before her parents' weddings), Serena's brother was in the hospital for an extended stay. She found that her family was very graceful during the difficult time. "My brother got really sick, and everything revolved around the hospital for over a year. My dad didn't work in the city anymore; everything changed. But even when my mom had a boyfriend or my dad had a girlfriend, everybody just rotated being with my brother. They wouldn't be there at the same time because that was awkward and uncomfortable, but they just agreed: my dad took these hours at the hospital, and Sandi would come with him, and my mom would take these hours, and I would come after school. They worked together. It wasn't super bad." The more people one asks to talk about their parents, the more answers one will get. Children of blended families go through many changes with their parents, which means we have a lot of opportunities to grow closer to them, or further apart. Our appreciation goes to parents who are sensitive to our needs and wants, who make an effort to include us in decisions, and who pay attention to the fact that we are struggling to fit into our new situations. However, we are able to forgive our parents when they make mistakes. We all have parents, and we all have different opinions about 'em. What do you want your children to say about you?

We're Still Brothers and Sisters

Our relationships with our siblings change over time, no matter what our family situation is. It can be difficult to understand what is affecting our connections with our brothers and sisters when, in addition to growing up, we are going through all the shifts of our blended families. Transitions like divorce and remarriage tend to shake up our relationships with our siblings, as they do the rest of our relationships. How exactly do the changes in our families affect our relationships with our siblings? Some children find themselves clinging to their sisters and brothers in the middle of the chaos, others find themselves alienated from their siblings when they want support, and still others feel that their relationships weren't affected much by their family's setup. Healthy sibling relationships take time and energy, just like all other familial bonds, and we find that in order to stay close to our brothers and sisters, regardless of whether they are half, step, or full, we have to be willing to put effort into the relationship, especially when the rest of our families are changing so much.

Just because they are related, brothers and sisters do not respond to their families the same way, even though they may have similar experiences. It is important for our parents to remember that because we are different people, our reactions to the shifts in our families may be very different. Alex remembers that he and his brother dealt with their uncomfortable family situation in two very different ways. "My dad is a super control freak. He has been like that ever since I can remember. I didn't know that I could refer to him as a control freak when I was younger, but that's what I've decided his problem is. The way I dealt with it as a kid was by nodding, doing a good job, and doing really well in school. I would say yes a lot and do what he said. The way my brother, Will, has dealt with it is by arguing. He was much more extroverted, whereas I was introverted. If I was disturbed about something, I wouldn't talk to anybody about it. I wouldn't say anything for days or weeks. Will would do the opposite, and so we didn't really help each other out at all. We had two different ways of dealing with the separation, divorce, and a family life that wasn't exactly terrific."

When we are young, we don't have the advantage of experience to be able to realize and understand differences like the one Alex described. We don't know or use categories such as introvert and extrovert, so we remain isolated. It is only when we are older, or when an older person helps us, that we understand that these differences are a fact of life, and that they can be overcome with some communication. Learning that our family members just deal with the world differently can do wonders for our relationships. It is the parents' and stepparents' job to look for such misunderstandings among their children (and among themselves) and help them learn to be sensitive to one another. Nothing can replace a close sibling relationship, and some siblings need a little help in getting there.

Some siblings find that their relationships only get closer during the chaos in their families. There are those of us who find that our sibling has an empathetic ear and makes a great confidante. Allison described how her relationship with her full sister was close because of their unstable family situation. "We were always a pair. I feel a lot of our relationship is directly based on the crazy family situation that we had. It was such total chaos, and the only person that I really knew would be there was Janet. The only one that she always knew would be there was me. So for a long time, a big part of our relationship was that we felt like these two drowning people clinging to each other in the sea. 'Who is at Mom's house? Well, we don't know. Who is at Dad's house? Well, we don't know. Where is Mom's house? We don't know. Where is Dad's house? We don't know. What's going on? Who is living there? What kind of dog do they have now?' Nothing was ever stable except that we were a pair. It was always The Girls together." That closeness has been invaluable to Allison, although she knows that because of the type of relationship that she and her sister have, growing up is just a little bit harder in some ways. She told us, "I was always protecting her, so we have gone through some of the phases that a child goes through in adolescence when they have to distance themselves from their parent. Janet and I went through some of those phases because she felt she had to say to me, 'I'm not you. I am different from you. I am good, even though I am not you,' at the exact same time that I was saying to my parents, 'I'm not you. I'm okay, even though I'm not you.' I would think, 'Of course you aren't me; hey, what's the matter with you?' We had this two-front War of Independence going on. Well, if you count our parents too, it was more like a four-front war."

Many of us, like Allison, find that we are drawn closer to our siblings during family crises or transitions because we are experiencing the same event at the same time. Lawrence's relationship with his sister has taken some turns since his parents' divorce. "In many ways, the changes in my family have created an opportunity for my sister and me to become closer. We can have conversations about what's going on, and we sort through the details of our family together. It's good for us." Zoe also mentioned that she is closer to her brother now because of how their family changed. "One thing I remember pretty clearly is that my relationship with my brother changed a lot because of our parents' divorce. My brother and I are really close in age. We grew up half fighting and half being friends. I remember that pretty quickly after our parents got separated and divorced, we got closer. We quit fighting and quit picking on each other and all that stuff. We needed each other to talk to about it. Out of all the family members, my relationship with him is the closest. I'm his only sibling. He talks to me a lot about his personal emotional life and all that stuff. He's not that open with everybody, but he is pretty open with me." It is clear from these stories that we value our siblings immeasurably.

Sometimes the most influential event in our relationship with our sibling is when one of us moves away from home. The events in our family may not bring us closer together, but usually once we have a little distance between us, we are better able to appreciate each other. Ben found that his home was much more peaceful after his sister left, which helped them become even closer. He gushed about his sister, "The last eighteen years of my life I've spent with her. She's just the most adorable thing you've ever seen. She moved out when she turned eighteen. And I was home by myself basically, which I didn't like, but it was a good thing because it eased the tension in my household. My mom and my sister just fought all the time. It was an everyday occurrence that while I was watching TV, I'd have to turn the volume up because of the shouting going over my head. When she left, that was over, which was really nice. The house got very quiet. It was definitely more civil when she was gone because the house rule became: 'All parties involved are going to lead separate lives.' My sister could visit who she wanted when she wanted, and that helped us all calm down." No one ever said living together is easy!

Our relationships with our half siblings change over time as well, and they have the added feature of being affected greatly by our family setup. Since Jordan's stepfather has left the picture, Jordan has become a father figure to his little half brother, who is fourteen years his junior. He told us, "We play all the time. I take him climbing. He's my big hiking partner. I help coach his sports teams. He likes me a lot. He probably thinks of me as his dad more than anybody else in his life. I don't know if you have to have just one person that you think of as your father figure, but of the men in his life I'm the probably the biggest figure. He'll fuss at my mom and not obey her, but when I come over he's good. He's moved a lot and seen a lot of different changes in his life. He is a pretty well-adapted kid." Jordan even sounded like a father, saying, "I try to teach him the proper way to deal with aggression and how to treat others. I try to work with him on issues of power and conflict. We deal with his problems with authority and with other kids. He's impatient. There's just got to be a little bit more discipline, but at the same time I don't want to stop his great energy. I'm going to make an NFL football player out of him. He's going to buy his mama a house!"

Stewart's brother looked out for him in much the same way as Jordan does for his brother. When parents seem unstable, having an older brother or sister to rely on is a great comfort for many children. Stewart told us, "My brother has always been my role model and the person I've looked up to in my life. He saw that I wasn't going to get the same upbringing he got with our father. He would always do sports with me, and he helped bring me up. I've always ridden my brother's coattails, my mom says. I work at the same company right now that my brother does. I am getting a computer and management degree, and my brother has a computer science degree. My brother and I are complete opposites in a lot of ways, but we are still best friends to this day." The pride and admiration in Jordan's and Stewart's voices when they talk about their brothers should put any parent at ease.

Relationships with half siblings are sometimes hard to define because of how large the age difference can be. Rebecca's relationships with her half sisters has changed with time. "I ended up taking care of them and being a type of baby-sitter for a while. I think that being responsible or taking care of them is a hard way to start out your relationship with your siblings. It has taken us a while to become peers, more equals in the family. Now one of them is in college, and I feel like we are definitely getting closer. When we were kids they were tight with each other and I was older. Then when Rose got a little older, she would talk to me about stuff that was going on in her life that she didn't want to tell our mom. That was the beginning of feeling a little bit closer to Rose, although it was still a slightly awkward position for me to be a pseudo-mom giving advice or something." Noticeably, Rebecca did not talk about the irritation of having two younger sisters following her around or getting into her things. Such childhood trials and tribulations fade as we mature, and we learn to cherish and respect our brothers and sisters.

But maybe our interviewees were a little too polite. Erica remembers the impact traveling between two homes had on her relationship with Vanessa. "When we were children, our dad really enjoyed taking us shopping. My mom does not enjoy it, and I always got the impression that she thought it was wrong or bad somehow to spend money on things you didn't really need. So when we would go shopping with my dad, I had no trouble buying what I needed, but I didn't want anything more. I thought

Vanessa should do the same, but instead she would sweet-talk our dad into buying her all kinds of junk. I felt like she was taking advantage of him and being wasteful and undisciplined, which made me very resentful toward her. I internalized my mom's attitude, and I would feel guilty when we would come back to her house with more new clothes. I know now that my dad enjoys buying things for us, that Vanessa was not manipulating him. I am sorry that our relationship suffered for so long because of those feelings. But Vanessa grew up to be a smart, caring, fun person, and now (luckily!) we are friends."

Vanessa also remembers that their family situation made her relationship with Erica more difficult for a number of years: "Erica was completely inaccessible to me for most of our childhood. I didn't feel that I could talk to her about anything because she would think I was irrational, melodramatic, and stupid. I felt that she was unaffected by our father's breakups, by our mother's remarriage, and by our half sister's birth, because we never talked to each other about how those events made us feel. We have been able to build a very caring friendship together, but for many years I felt estranged from her because of how differently we handled our emotions." This is another instance in which a little understanding that other people have different perceptions of the same situation turned a contentious relationship into a warm one.

When siblings are farther apart in age, like Rebecca and her half sisters, they may avoid many of the scrapes same-age siblings get into. In fact, Margarita told us that her younger half sister is the person she is closest to in her family, even though she is only nine. She describes what will happen when her younger sister becomes a teenager: "My mother can't deal very well with teenage girls. She will talk to me about how she doesn't want to raise another teenager. I think it's because she had a really difficult adolescence. She read too much Sylvia Plath or something." So Margarita's solution is to live with her sister herself! "I've decided that when I'm in graduate school, my little sister will come live with me. She'll be about thirteen. I'll take her to class with me. She's smart as a tack. We're very close, and I think it would be better for her to live with me than with our mom. I keep telling my parents that. I say, 'If she gets bored or something, you just send her up here. She can come to my classes and help me get better grades.'" No doubt most parents wouldn't mind shipping their thirteen-year-olds off to live with a big sister!

A large age difference is just one of the many factors that influences our relationships with our siblings and half siblings. Hazel described her relationships with her sisters, separating her own experience from what "normal" families go through: "In the real world, six years apart is a pretty big age difference. In my world, though, my younger sister was really close in age to me, because my older sister is eleven years older. It is going to be really interesting to see how my relationship with my younger sister develops as she gets older. She is already starting to be a lot more of a freethinking person. We sit and talk together in a way that I wish I had with my older sister."

Whatever our situation is, our siblings are part of our family, and our relationships with them are affected by family transitions. Some of us are very close right from the start, providing one another with an ally amidst difficult changes. Many of us need the distance of separate residences and a few years under our belts in order to appreciate one another. Brothers and sisters are special people, because they are the only ones who know the same family we know, from a similar perspective. When we can learn to understand and respect one another, these friendships can be some of the most important in our lives.

Reflections and Advice

Just because a child grows up doesn't mean that she is no longer a part of her family. We are still children of divorce, children of remarriage, stepchildren, and half siblings, even after we are old enough to have families of our own. One thing that does come with age is perspective, and though we are still members of our families after we grow up, we are removed from them enough to comment on how they have affected us. Our looking back can be nerve-racking for parents, but in order to help other families avoid the mistakes we made, we have to admit we made them in the first place. Happily, we can also teach by example. We remember the ways our families supported us, made us feel safe, and taught us important life lessons.

Drawing from our experiences, we can offer suggestions on how to build a blended family that can cooperate and thrive.

When we have two households to compare, it is easier for us to put a finger on the family patterns that don't work for us. We can see how each of our homes handles particular issues, and we can decide which method feels better to us. When our parents remarry, we are instantly confronted with the differences between our old household and our new ones, because we are watching our parents behave in a new relationship. We notice the ways in which our stepparent is different from our biological parent. Lawrence was confronted with an enormous shift in the level of communication that happened in his household when his father got remarried. "My parents would require that we go to bed if they were going to argue. I'm glad I didn't ever watch them fight, but the problem was that I was perceiving their relationship as normal and healthy, and that wasn't what was going on. They are both passive-aggressive and don't like to confront anyone, much less each other. My siblings and I rarely saw any anger or frustration. I think one nice thing about my father's side of the family now is that my stepmom is really up-front and frank. Things don't go unsaid. That's certainly much more helpful than before." We cannot stress enough how important it is for parents to tell children what is appropriate for their age and to be honest with them about what is happening in their families.

When both of our parents are remarried, we notice the differences in our two stepparents' abilities to communicate and interact with us. Zoe felt that she was better able to build a relationship with her stepmother, and she explained the reasons why she did not connect as well with her stepfather: "The biggest difference between my stepparents was that my stepmom perceived me as a kid going through a lot of really difficult stuff. My stepdad perceived me as a threat to his wife's well-being, happiness, and everything else. In my perspective his communication skills lacked a little bit, and so did his willingness to get to know me or to perceive me as the fourteen-year-old girl that I was. I think he saw me as being much stronger than I was. He thought I was more influential in our family situation, and he didn't recognize that I really was an upset girl. And I definitely was a girl, not an adult at all at the time. There were mean names flying out of his mouth, things that shouldn't have been said to a kid. So, of course, I said things that you shouldn't say to anyone." While children's opinions need to be respected, parents and stepparents need not to forget that we are still children. We are no match for adults in emotional competitions because we simply do not have the experience or the tools to draw from. When a child acts out, she is expressing a need for guidance and attention.

Paradoxically, stepparents often perceive their spouse's children as the authority on whether or not they will be accepted into the family, while children often feel that their opinions and feelings are not being heard.

When a stepparent enters the picture, the tantrums and crankiness so many parents experience with their children is often our way of getting listened to. A child's opinion is easily disregarded, which is a grave mistake if that child is to be content and happy in his new family situation. We make it through transitions faster and smoother if we are given room to express how those transitions make us feel.

Feeling that our voices are not being heard is not the only adverse reaction we have to some of our parents' behavior. Sometimes instead of wishing we had more clout, we wish we didn't have to be the responsible one. Many of our interviewees likened the experience of having both parents in the same room to being a baby-sitter. Jay talked about how his family works now: "I think it is really sad that my father and mother can't get along at all. They are two really wonderful people, but when they get around each other it just doesn't work. Something just happens and they both turn into children. I wish that didn't happen." Many of us feel that we must mediate, translate, or relay information between our parents, which is usually one of our least favorite things to do. We are not messengers; we are not allies on any particular side of a battle. Many parents make the mistake of believing us to be an impartial audience, at whom they may direct the aggression they feel toward their ex-spouse. We ask parents not to do that. When feeling intense anger towards an ex-spouse, do not vent it at your children. In that situation, find someone else to talk to, and protect your children from the pain of choosing a side. Our parents need to understand that when they do not deal civilly with each other, we are disappointed and exasperated by both of them.

Sometimes our parents don't listen to us, sometimes they lay all of their complaints upon us, sometimes they do all sorts of things we find ineffective and unconstructive. Even when we are making the effort to get along, we need to remember that change is a slow process. Martin commented, "I have to say it's very, very hard to get used to, especially if you're young. Suddenly all these new people appear in your life, and you don't know what to do with them. It was hard for me just to get used to the idea that suddenly my family was actually two families. I don't think that my parents really appreciated how much of an effect it really had on me. It made me a lot more quiet and reflective. It just made me think that the world was a lot different place then I thought it would be."

The silver lining, of course, is that we learn from our parents' mistakes. Jordan carefully watched his mother relate to his former stepfather and was able to say this about it: "I think it influenced me a lot more than I want to admit. I certainly learned a lot about choices regarding drugs, anger, and ways of dealing with difficult situations. My mom should have gotten out earlier. I learned about when to stop giving yourself in support for somebody else. There has got to be a separation between you and the other person. You can't try to save somebody like my mom did. I will never ever repeat that or wish it on anyone. We all came out of it a little bit jaded, but that's the world." We learn, and we move on with our lives.

All parents make mistakes. Thankfully, most of those mistakes are forgivable, and they don't portend the end of the world. Meredith explained it this way: "I turned out okay. I don't know what about me could be different. I can't go back and say, 'Well, if you had been more considerate here and here and here, I would be different.' Perhaps I would have grown up less compassionate or snotty or not as self-reliant or not as confident or something like that. So, whatever my parents did wrong, I can vouch for one thing that they did right, and that's me. Nothing else matters, because I am pretty much okay, and I like me. Probably the best measure of a parent is whether or not their child has the capacity for enjoyment, the capacity for love and kindness, whether they are happy, and whether they are good. I am all those things, so they really couldn't have screwed up that badly."

To their credit, many parents work exceptionally hard at creating family environments where we can grow up safe and happy. A blended family is one of the hardest types to keep healthy because there is so much communicating to be done. We understand that and appreciate the parents and stepparents who devote their energies to our well-being. Serena has an extremely sunny view of her family because they all were able to work together. She told us, "We're 'the clan.' I guess we are like the Brady Bunch when all of us kids are together, because there are two from my mom and four from my stepdad, so that is six of us, and we get along pretty well. Everybody laughs about how it works out. When people meet my family and my stepfamily, they are always amazed that it is as comfortable as it is. It could be so uncomfortable, and it isn't. We just treat one another like human beings."

For Derek, the fact that his family was such a difficult place to be actually had its merits because it taught him resilience: "I'd say one thing that was important was just the strength of character that really came through in my family members when it was needed. It was a lesson about 'whatever doesn't kill you really makes you stronger.' That's something that's been driven into me."

Although there is no foolproof formula that produces a perfectly happy, functional, communicating family, there are some common threads among the people who feel that their families work well. Rebecca put it best when she told her own story: "My dad worked really hard to keep in touch with me, and both my parents made decisions mutually and presented a united front to me about stuff. Basically the idea was, 'We're your parents. And we both love you, and we are always going to be your parents and both care about you, and we expect you to love both of us.'" Jay also captured the essence of our message when asked what it was that his stepmother did right. He replied instantly, "She loved me right through it. She didn't stop caring."

What do all of our experiences, reflections, insights, and memories have in common? They make us feel that we have good advice to give! We speculate that many new stepparents just want a how-to manual, and while we have made it clear that every family is different, our interviewees had strong opinions about what is best to do and not to do when becoming a blended family. Of course, our prescriptions are drawn directly from what we went through personally, but considering that we all went through the transition from "normal" family to complex, intricate, confusing family, we feel that our advice is sound and should be heeded. Here is the advice we have to give.

Allison found that her stepmother was usually worried about her, which made their relationship decidedly strained. She told us, "Because my stepmom's a counselor, she was always on an eagle-sharp lookout for upcoming symptoms of my deep anxiety, 'Trauma Childhood Syndrome.' I'd just be cranky that day because they had served us meat loaf at lunch, but she always thought I had a huge emotional complex. Probably, the thing that I'd say the most is wait for a problem to come up before you start freaking out about it. My advice would be to make sure that if anyone is freaking out, it's the kid. This one person can do the freaking out for everybody. Kids will make sure that you understand that they're not happy with what's going on, but not everything they do is a manifestation of their unhappiness. When sitting at the dinner table, instead of thinking, 'Oh, look how fast she is chewing; maybe this is hidden aggression,' leave me alone; I'm just hungry."

One thing many stepchildren would like to say to stepparents is "Don't move in too quickly!" We need to grieve the end of our old family before we are ready to accept a new configuration. We need to trust that our stepparent is a good person before we will accept any authority from them. We need to feel that our opinion is respected before we are willing to change it. Hazel put it this way: "I would say to try and remember that kids are people with very clear-cut thought patterns and feelings. Don't try to impose your world without thinking about how they are going to react to that. It is important to be really sympathetic and to put yourself in their shoes before you do anything that might really affect them. Try and wade in instead of diving in. After I had been living with my stepmom for a while, she could tell me to do the dishes or pick something up, whereas I think it would have been a problem if she had just moved right in and done that." Mark also feels that the best way to start a stepfamily is to just ease into it slowly. He told us, "Don't try too hard. I always think that's a big thing, because when there's too much effort, it just becomes smothering. You don't want someone that doesn't know you to start acting like they are your parent right away. Just ease into it. Just try to be their friend more than their parent. Let the parent do the work with them. Realize that a good biological parent and a kid are going to need some time alone."

For stepparents who view children as an obstacle to be overcome, Greg has this to say: "If you are getting married, you need to decide whether it is going to be a permanent thing, and if it is, you are marrying their family, too. People don't just marry individual other people;

they marry into other lives. It's too bad when some parents marry and the kids get a stepdad who doesn't consider the stepchildren part of the family. It's sad when he thinks they are just things that get in the way of his time with his new wife. I just don't think that sort of thing ever really works out."

So how does a stepparent ease into a relationship with us? Jordan has a few ideas: "Show interest in the kids. Do the things they enjoy. Encourage them in the things they are good at. Don't try to be their parent too quickly. Don't try to be too pushy about it. Just be their friend. Over time, as they get to know you, they will see your good qualities. You'll grow together if it's meant to be. If they see you making their mother or their father happy, and everybody is getting along, slowly, I think, you'll overcome whatever difficulties are there. It's not the structural problem of an outsider coming in and taking the place of another person or inserting themselves into your life. It's the content of the person, not the form of the situation. I don't think there is anything structurally weird about that type of relationship for the children. Kids are adaptable little people. They really are. I could have happily accepted Paul as a father figure if he wasn't Paul!" Ben echoed Jordan's point. His advice was: "At first, they should just try to be a friend, reach the kids on their level. After a while, if their relationship with the child becomes serious and they become an adult figure in the household, they are going to have to take on some sort of a parenting role. I would say try to make that as much a mentor-ship as possible. For kids, the feeling of having this foreign person come in and become a task-master is awful, but having a person come in and be a good guiding influence is awesome. I think that a steppar-ent can at times play the disciplinary role, if they're also being guiding and helpful. There is a balance that every family has to find."

Stewart said, "My advice to stepparents is: If the kids are paying a lot of attention to you and hanging around you a lot, then pay attention to them. Pay attention, but don't force yourself on them. If they ask for something, help them out. Do little things for them. Those are the things they are going to remember later on." Getting to know kids is not rocket science; it takes skills we all have. We just have to remember to use them. It is important for parents and stepparents to remember that we are able to adjust to whatever our family will be, we just need some time and support. The mere existence of a stepparent is not a problem. What affects us is who they are, and how they treat us.

Stepparents aren't the only people who make up our blended families, and we have advice for our biological parents, too! Tanya had this to say about how to treat children after big changes in a family's structure: "Never let kids think that you don't care about them or that you don't love them. Whatever it takes to remind them of how important they are to you, you have to do it. That's the biggest thing. Even though you are moving apart, you still need to give your kids the same attention you would if you were still living with them. Always make sure that they know that you're there for them. Otherwise the relationship just falls apart." We need to be listened to. We need to be reassured that we do not lose any love from our parents just because someone else is entering the family.

Derek touched upon another important issue while talking about divorce. He wants to say to parents, "You don't have to love each other. Just be decent to each other." It is not usually the case that we wish our parents would get back together. We don't feel that it is necessary for them to be in love. We do, however, want them to be able to deal with each other maturely. That means leaving us out of their battles, learning to talk to each other civilly, and never asking us to take sides.

Parents who have difficulty dealing with each other usually find a sore spot when they start talking about finances. A blended family's money is a very complicated, emotionally charged issue. Jordan mentioned, "I know a lot of my development and my social views and my political views stem from that time. I came out of the relationship understanding how deeply it depended upon economics. I can imagine a much different family life if our money situation was okay. I want to tell people to get rich first. Have money before you have kids." Or, know how to handle what money you have, so that you don't place the burden of it on your children.

We know that being related by blood does not mean we will feel an intense emotional connection. We have seen how much personality plays a part in our compatibility with stepparents, half siblings, biological parents, or anyone else. Greg, whose mother and father remarried each other after years of being divorced, gave us a poignant example of how complex family relationships are and how we can never take them for granted. He told us, "I think we all had an idea that we were going to be a perfect family. We were all going to pick up the roles of husband, wife, and son. We were going to act them out in the way that we saw them on TV or something, but it always seemed like we didn't know our roles as family members. We all were thrown in together again, and we were genetically supposed to be certain people, but none of us remembered exactly how to do it."

In general, we understand that our parents get divorced and remarried because it makes them happier, healthier people, and we ultimately support it, even if it is a difficult transition for us to make. Sometimes our support takes a long time to surface, but the more distance we gain from our childhoods, the more we are able to understand why our parents do what they do. In fact, we often find that our families change for the better, eventually. When asked if having better relationships made her mother and father better parents, Zoe responded emphatically, "Oh my God. Yes."

Blended families are growing in number very quickly. For many of us, the stigma attached to divorce just wasn't in existence anymore once we were old enough to notice, because so many of our friends came from families with single parents, remarried parents and so forth. With the added fact that whatever one grows up with is "normal," we usually don't feel that we belong to any special group. In fact, one of the more telling statements came from our interview with Zoe. We asked her how it felt as a child to come from a nontraditional family, and she responded, "Did I not have a traditional family?"

Our Top Ten Guidelines

We have heard many stories, opinions, and points of view on countless issues that are material to blended families. This is our summary list of the ten most important guidelines we can draw from our experience and our interviews.

1. *Children are not adults.* We need to have the relationships and changes in our families explained to us. We are not stupid, but we do not have past experience to draw from. When very young, we may not know what a marriage means, let alone a divorce. We may not know what a half sister is or how she will affect us. Of course, the older we get, the more we are able to figure out on our own. But at any age we need our parents to be candid about what is going on.

2. *Children are still people.* We don't have adult-sized responsibilities, but we do have adult-sized reactions, feelings, and opinions. We need respect, just like any other individual. When important decisions must be made, we need to know that our voice counts.

3. *We all have our own ways of dealing with the changes in our families.* Even very close siblings don't have the same reactions to the same experiences. We all have unique personalities and points of view.

3. *Genetic ties don't determine a family.* We love the people who treat us well, who support us, who stand by us, and who care for us. We don't have a love quota system

calling for only two full-time parents; we have room in our hearts for many.

4. *Both sides of our family are important to us.* We are severely affected by parents badmouthing each other or competing for our time and attention. We need our family to understand that our other household is part of our life, too.

5. *Expect a period of adjustment.* Some period of adjustment is normal when we are traveling back and forth and especially when a very large transition, like a remarriage (or adolescence!) has taken place. We'll get used to it. Excuse occasional crabbiness.

6. *Good communication is the key.* Big news, medium-sized news, or small news—tell us. It is important that we know what is going on. Tell your ex-spouse information that affects them, like plans to move. Keeping everyone informed is the best way to avoid misunderstanding. The more honest and up front we can be with one another, the better off we are.

7. *Money is not the problem.* The way family members treat one another when dealing with money issues is the problem. We don't like watching our parents turn into ogres when the child support is due. In fact, in most cases, our message to parents about money is "Grow Up!" Our parents' fears about money need not be our crosses to bear.

8. *Our families are normal to us.* We are flexible, especially as young children. We are resilient and able to weather enormous transitions in our families. Our family

arrangements are second nature to us, even if they are not ideal.

9. *Stepparents aren't parents.* They really are different, and for each stepchild they need to tailor a new role that works for them. When building trust, build slowly. For most older children, a stepparent is most positively influential as a friend, not a disciplinarian. Finding the right niche for a stepparent takes patience and effort, from everyone involved. It's worth it.

10. *Everything changes when we move out of the house.* Childhood doesn't last forever, and when we are on our own, we have an entirely new perspective on our families, as they do on us. The roughness of adolescence can be smoothed out by a little distance, and often we find ourselves thinking more objectively about how our families worked. Everyday irritations give way to a larger appreciation of who our family members are and why we love them. It is difficult to remember when a child is nine years old and screaming, "You're not even my real mom!" that someday he will appreciate all his stepmother has done for him, but usually, it is true.

Blended families push some of our biggest emotional buttons: they test our loyalties, make us face our fears about money, challenge us to be flexible, and work best when we can communicate what we need and want. Our family is the environment where we learn the most about how to treat other people. That fact alone should push all parents to work as hard as they can to give their children an honest atmosphere in which they can be heard, valued, and treated with respect. We have room in our hearts and lives for stepparents, for half siblings, for stepsiblings, for stepgrandparents, for stepcousins, for half nieces, and for any family member who makes an effort to get to know us individually. Sometimes we have to grow up and out of our resistance to the transitions in our family, but when we feel loved, we will reciprocate with love: it is that simple.

Acknowledgments

First and foremost, we would like to extend a special thanks to the many people we interviewed. Thank you for your time, your patience, and your insights. Your memories are invaluable, and we are sincerely grateful that you chose to share them with us.

We are deeply indebted to all our friends at Reed College in Portland, Oregon. Thanks to our professors, for teaching us how to write in the first place, and for being supportive even when it seemed impossible that we would be able to write a book and finish our school assignments in the same decade. And thanks to all of the friends who supported us during the writing of the book.

Thank you to our housemate, Jennifer, and all the guys who were at the big house on Gladstone over the summer, for letting us talk incessantly about the breakthroughs we were having, for wonderful insights, and for making us food. Thanks especially to Gabriel for being the computer fix-it guy, the barbecue guy, and the lets-go-see-a-movie guy when we were working all day every day.

We would like to thank the staff of the Sylvia Beach Hotel in Newport, Oregon, especially Goody Cable, for allowing us to work in the dining room after hours, and for getting us big towels when we ran into the ocean in our clothes after writing the initial book proposal.

We extend enormous thanks to the staff of Wildcat Canyon Press, who invest so much of themselves in the beautiful books they produce. A special thank you goes to Julie for the initial idea and creative boost behind this project. Thank you Tamara for your support, professional and otherwise, and for the way you call us "the Authors" when we visit the office.

Were we to try and enumerate the reasons why we need to thank Roy M. Carlisle, our editor, readers would never be able to finish these acknowledgments. So instead, we will quietly remove our hats and whisper "thank you" to the man who really made this book a reality for us. We love you.

Vanessa would like to personally thank Susan Kennedy, for always believing, no, assuming, that I would write a book, even when I wasn't writing one. Thanks to Melissa, Nicholas, Cecily, Jessie, Jessica, and Sean for the incredible support you have been, and your long-distance phone calls, for your concern, for your challenges, and for your faith in me, through everything. You know how long I would like to praise you all. All styles of gratitude to Erica Celeste, for never making me feel guilty for sleeping late, for being my emotional support during some grand tumult, and for being the best older sister and coauthor on the planet (or in space!).

Erica would like to personally thank Vanessa Dawn for her unceasing hard work. When I thought it wouldn't get done, she pulled through. From four interviews a day, to turning hazy thoughts into concrete words on paper, she continually made it happen. I am proud to have such a wonderful, bright sister. And to Gabriel who listened and understood, who gave me support, encouragement, and friendship. Thank you for all we have shared. I am so lucky to share this moment in space and time with you.

Last but most important, we would like to thank our whole blended family—Roy, our dad; Chris, our mom; Jim, our stepdad; and Kelsey, our sister—for their unending support of our project, even when it meant that we were telling the world about their stories too. Your excitement and involvement in this book, when offering memories, giving us hugs, or rereading a manuscript, have reminded us again of your amazing loyalty to us. We love you.

About the Authors

Erica is working on a Ph.D. in Cognitive Psychology at Princeton University and has a B.A. from Reed College. In her spare time she likes to read science fiction and real science, listen to jazz, dance, and cook. She harbors a dream of one day seeing the earth from space—perhaps being the first psychologist on Mars!

Vanessa attends Reed College where she is majoring in Psychology. Usually, she can be found in the Hauser Library hunched over schoolbooks, or in a downstairs dance studio, belly dancing to a different drum. Her previous accomplishments involve surviving adolescence, achieving close, loving relationships with her parents, and becoming a volunteer mentor to preteen girls who are struggling to do the same.

Wildcat Canyon Press publishes books that embrace such subjects as friendship, spirituality, women's issues, and home and family, all with a focus on self-help and personal growth. Great care is taken to create books that inspire reflection and improve the quality of our lives. Our books invite sharing and are frequently given as gifts.

For a catalog of our publications, please write:

Wildcat Canyon Press
2716 Ninth Street
Berkeley, California 94710
Phone: (510) 848-3600
Fax: (510) 848-1326
info@wildcatcanyon.com

More Wildcat Canyon Titles ...

THOSE WHO CAN...TEACH!: CELEBRATING TEACHERS WHO MAKE
A DIFFERENCE
A tribute to our nation's teachers!
Lorraine Glennon and Mary Mohler
$12.95 ISBN 1-885171-35-8

A COUPLE OF FRIENDS: THE REMARKABLE FRIENDSHIP BETWEEN
STRAIGHT WOMEN AND GAY MEN
What makes the friendships between straight women and gay men so
wonderful? Find out in this honest and fascinating book.
Robert H. Hopcke and Laura Rafaty
$14.95 ISBN 1-885171-33-1

STILL FRIENDS: LIVING HAPPILY EVER AFTER (EVEN IF YOUR MARRIAGE
FALLS APART)
True stories of couples who have managed to keep their friendships
intact after splitting up.
Barbara Quick
$12.95 ISBN 1-885171-36-6

girlfriends: INVISIBLE BONDS, ENDURING TIES
Filled with true stories of ordinary women and extraordinary friend-
ships, *girlfriends* has become a gift of love among women everywhere.
Carmen Renee Berry and Tamara Traeder
$13.95 ISBN 1-885171-08-0
Also Available: Hardcover gift edition, $20.00 ISBN 1-885171-20-X

girlfriends TALK ABOUT MEN: SHARING SECRETS FOR A GREAT
RELATIONSHIP
This book shares insights from real women in real relationships—not
just from the "experts."
Carmen Renee Berry and Tamara Traeder
$14.95 ISBN 1-885171-21-8

girlfriends FOR LIFE

This follow-up to the best-selling *girlfriends* is an all-new collection of stories and anecdotes about the amazing bonds of women's friendships.
Carmen Renee Berry and Tamara Traeder
$13.95 ISBN 1-885171-32-3

AUNTIES: OUR OLDER, COOLER, WISER FRIENDS
An affectionate tribute to the unique and wonderful women we call "Auntie."
Tamara Traeder and Julienne Bennett
$12.95 ISBN 1-885171-22-6

THE COURAGE TO BE A STEPMOM: FINDING YOUR PLACE WITHOUT LOSING YOURSELF
Hands-on advice and emotional support for stepmothers.
Sue Patton Thoele
$14.95 ISBN 1-885171-28-5

CELEBRATING FAMILY
True stories about how baby boomers have recognized the flaws of their families and come to love them as they are.
Lisa Braver Moss
$13.95 ISBN 1-885171-30-7

INDEPENDENT WOMEN: CREATING OUR LIVES, LIVING OUR VISIONS
How women value independence and relationship and are redefining their lives to accommodate both.
Debra Sands Miller
$16.95 ISBN 1-885171-25-0

THE WORRYWART'S COMPANION: TWENTY-ONE WAYS TO SOOTHE YOURSELF AND WORRY SMART
The perfect gift for anyone who lies awake at night worrying.
Dr. Beverly Potter
$11.95 ISBN 1-885171-15-3

Books are available at fine bookstores nationwide.

Prices subject to change without notice